LORD, LIFT ME UP …
Beyond the Tumult of the Times

Bruce Monroe Morgan

*"And I, when I am lifted up from the earth, will draw
all people to myself" (John 12:32)*

Published in the United States by Nurturing Faith Inc., Macon GA,
www.nurturingfaith.net.

Library of Congress Cataloging-in-Publication Data is available.

ISBN 978-1-938514-12-8

Most scripture quotations are taken from the *New King James Version*®, copyright © 1982
by Thomas Nelson, Inc., used by permission; all rights reserved. Where indicated, scripture
quotations are taken from the *New American Standard Bible*®, copyright © 1960, 1962, 1963,
1968, 1971, 1972, 1973, 1975, 1977, 1995 by The Lockman Foundation, used by permission.
Author's paraphrasing may apply in some quotations.

Chapter 19, "Beyond the Dogs of War . . . Private Ryan and the Young Prince of Glory," first
appeared in *Pulpit Digest*, vol. 81, no. 2 (April-June 2000): 27-33.

Dedicated to Emma Peck Morgan,
whose love and encouragement are boundless

CONTENTS

PREFACE

For more than 150 years, in season and out of season, the hand on the steeple of the First Baptist Church of Griffin, Georgia, has "silently spoken to the world about us of the glory of the other world."[1] The origin of the icon remains unknown.

Lightning struck the church steeple in 1884, and the church minutes record for June 8 that year: "On motion the deacons were requested to look after and have the lightning rod repaired."[2]

During the repairs workmen discovered that the lightning rod was a large hand with the index finger pointing heavenward. The hand on the steeple had become so corroded, it was unrecognizable by the church members on the ground. Therefore, one bolt of lightning had restored the elevation of the hand and rekindled the aspiration of Johnson Oatman's hymn, "Higher Ground":

> I want to scale the utmost height
> And catch a gleam of glory bright;
> But still I'll pray till heav'n I've found,
> "Lord, lead me on to higher ground."
>
> Lord, lift me up and let me stand,
> By faith on heaven's table land,
> A higher plane than I have found;
> Lord, plant my feet on higher ground.

This book is an answer to the prayer and an anthem of gratitude to the ministers, deacons, and company, both present and departed, of that august household of faith in which I was privileged to serve for more than three decades.

I wish to thank the following persons whose skills contributed to the publication of this book:

- Sandy Cropsy, a playwright, and Joy Durham Barrett, a novelist, are mentors from whom I have learned.
- Jan Hensley, a graphic artist, designed the steeple on page ix.
- Ruth Morgan Reynolds and Reid Reynolds provided critical technical and clerical assistance.
- Nathan and Lisa Morgan offered valuable insights.
- Colleagues Jim Rogers, Sandra Hogue, and William Coates Jr., my pastor, gave valued suggestions and words of encouragement.
- Erin Barnett served as art consultant.

Notes

[1]John H. Goddard, Jr., *History of the First Baptist Church of Griffin, Georgia 1841-1977* (Atlanta: Cherokee Publishing Co., 1978), 56.

[2]Ibid., 27.

Original etching by Lucile Flemister (1895-1995).
Archives, First Baptist Church, Griffin, Georgia.

The Transfiguration
Raphael, 1519-20
Pictures courtesy of the Bridgeman Art Library.

CHAPTER 1

BEYOND DIMNESS ...
Look Up!

Luke 9:28-36

The exclamation "Behold" became a characteristic way of introducing a story in the Gospels, being used sixty-two times in Matthew and fifty-seven times in Luke with the force of "Pay close attention" or "Be sure to look at this."

—*William E. Hull* [1]

Raphael's last painting, *The Transfiguration,* portrays in the upper half of the canvas the glorification of Christ before the awestruck disciples—Peter, James, and John. Matthew calls the change in Jesus' appearance a metamorphosis: "His face shone like the sun, and his garments became as white as light" (Matt. 17:2 NASB). Mark calls the change a metaphor: "His garments became radiant and exceedingly white, as no launderer on earth can whiten them" (Mark 9:3 NASB). Luke calls the change a mystery: "His face became different" (Luke 9:29 NASB), and mortal eyes suddenly saw "the glory of the coming of the Lord!"

But in the lower half of the canvas a distraught father appears with his epileptic son, whose affliction the remaining disciples are helpless to cure. There, all eyes are focused downward on the stricken child, but all hands are pointing upward toward the resplendent Christ. Raphael in oils and Luke in words accent the text, "This is my son, my chosen one" (Luke 9:35 NASB).

Pay close attention to this! Theologians use the phrase "prevenient grace," which is grace going before or preceding an event. The transfiguration of Jesus records a prevenient experience of resurrection glory prior to the darkness at Calvary. The message of both artist and evangelist is "Look up!"

Dead Men Talking

Look up! What do you see? I see dead men talking. Moses the lawgiver and Elijah the prophet, dead and gone for centuries, are talking intensely with Jesus. What are they talking about? Exodus! They are talking with Jesus about his approaching exodus from Jerusalem. Both Moses and Elijah are authorities on exodus—the way out. Moses, with his rod, struck the Red Sea and the waters parted and formed a pathway through which the Hebrew people passed toward the land of promise (Exod. 14:15-16).

Elijah, with his mantle, struck the Jordan River and crossed dry-shod toward the waiting chariots of fire that gathered him into glory (2 Kings 2:8). Soon, Jesus in Jerusalem will take up his cross, wade through "death's cold sullen stream" where he will strike a fatal blow against humankind's last enemy: Death is swallowed up in victory (1 Cor. 15:54b).

Such boundary experiences between the living and the dead stretch our imaginations, sometimes beyond belief. Poets speak of "intimations of immortality"[2] in nature, but saints report glimpses of glory from the valley of the shadows.

The story is told of "Doctor Henry," who was affectionately known "as the dean of black preaching" in Chattanooga. He was a patriarchal pastor, civic leader, and wise friend. When his beloved wife was suddenly stricken with illness, he spent every hour near her in the intensive care unit. In the dawn's early light of her last day, she awakened him as he lay nearby on the fold-up cot: "Henry, wake up! Do you see those people yonder? They look familiar." "No, Honey," he replied, "I don't see anything." She responded, "You will, you will!"

Her words recall Jesus' teaching in the temple about the future: "When these things begin to take place, straighten up and lift up your heads because your redemption is drawing near" (Luke 21:28 NASB).

Sleeping Men Awaking

Look up! What do you see? I see sleeping men awakening, who "know the time, that is already the hour . . . to awaken from sleep" (Rom. 13:11). Sleep has been called a passive act of disobedience to the command of Jesus, "Watch and pray."[3] The spirit is willing, but the flesh remains weak. The pillar apostles are consistently and honestly portrayed as overcome with sleep.

In colonial Virginia before the advent of the interstate highway system, every other boarding house and bed and breakfast inn featured a sign in front: "George Washington Slept Here!" Someone estimated that if the father of our country had slept in every bed that claimed his occupancy, he would have slept through the American Revolution.

On Mount Tabor the apostles almost slept through the transfiguration of Christ. Later, they did sleep through his ordeal in Gethsemane, evoking his anguished question: "Could you not watch with me for one hour?" (Mark 14:37).

Do you remember the little prayer you learned at your mother's knee?

> Now I lay me down to sleep,
> I pray the Lord my soul to keep.
> May angels keep me through the night,
> And wake me in the morning light.[4]

This prayer awakens wisdom from the mouth of babes (Ps. 9:2). What if I should die before I wake? What if I should sleepwalk through life and never hear the trumpet call to watch and pray? And yet, some souls are awakened from their preoccupation with temporal concerns by a sudden and shattering experience.

Once, when a man was walking down a Boston street, a sudden gust of wind off the North Atlantic lifted a stone cross from a downtown church and sent it crashing into the pavement, just inches in front of the man's feet, whereupon he looked up and exclaimed: "I have seen the Lord!"[5] Even the wind sometimes whispers "Look Up!"

No Tabernacles Please

But while a sudden or shattering religious experience can be recollected, it cannot be frozen in time or space. Thus, Peter's proposal to construct three tabernacles—one for Moses, one for Elijah, and one for Jesus—is unworthy of an answer. Peter's construction might have created at Mount Tabor another Mount Rushmore like the one in the black hills of South Dakota, with the heads of Presidents Washington, Jefferson, and Lincoln carved in stone and sixty feet in height. But such a memorial would not have become a sanctuary for saints but possibly a Mecca for tourists, complete with ski lift, camera shop, and Starbucks.

Tabernacles cannot confine or contain the glory of God. Had Peter forgotten the story of the old Tabernacle at Shiloh, the Tent of Meeting where the glory of the Lord once filled the place and the Ark of the Covenant with its Ten Commandments guaranteed the power and presence of God? But no one has God in a box! Alas, the day came when the glory of the Lord appeared no more at Shiloh. The Ark of the Covenant was stolen by the Philistines, and the shocking news sent the wife of one of the priests into premature labor, and the hapless child was named Ichabod—meaning "the glory has departed" (1 Sam. 4:19-22).

The glory of God is always on the go. Missionary E. Stanley Jones tells of a fort in India that required 4,000 guards per shift daily, but the city it was built to guard had long ago moved miles away![6] This is the fate of tabernacles, forts, and religious monuments. The essence of their inspiration remains forever illusive.

One Solitary Man Remaining

Soon the epiphany on the mountain dissipates like drifting fog across the valley. Dead men talking are struck dumb with silence. A voice from the cloud finally breaks the silence: "This is my son, my chosen one; listen to him" (Luke 9:35 NASB). After the voice from beyond has spoken, Jesus is found alone.

Jesus remains alone: In the wedding ceremony the minister sometimes quotes the Psalmist, "God sets the solitary in families" (Ps. 68:6). But on the mountain of glory, God set the universe in the solitary. Listen to him.

Jesus remains alone: "The law was given through Moses, but grace and truth came through Jesus Christ" (John 1:17). Listen to him.

Jesus remains alone: "All things have been created through him and for him. He is before all things, and in him all things hold together" (Col. 1:16-17 NASB). Listen to him.

Jesus remains alone: Pay close attention to him, because the mind of Christ is the very mind of God.

In *Our Town*, Thornton Wilder records a conversation between teenagers, George and Rebecca, about a letter Jane Crofut received from her minister. It was addressed in this manner: "Jane Crofut; The Crofut

Farm; Grover's Corners; Sutton County; New Hampshire; United States of America." "What's so funny about that?" asks George. "But wait a minute," Rebecca responds. "That's not all: United States of America . . . Continent of North America; Western Hemisphere; the Earth; the Solar System; the Universe; the mind of God.""What do you know!" sighs George. "What do you know!" "And the postman brought it just the same," says Rebecca.[7]

The mind of God, containing the mysteries of the universe, was once written on a frail envelope of human flesh (John 1:14). It was labeled: "General Delivery; Bethlehem of Judea; In the Days of Herod the King; In the Reign of Caesar Augustus." And the postman brought it just the same. And even more remarkable, the letter is addressed to you. What do you know! What do you know!

A Prayer

> I ask no dream, no prophet ecstasies,
> No sudden rending of the veil of clay,
> No angel visitant, no opening skies;
> But take the dimness of my soul away.
> Amen.

—George Crowly[8]

Notes

[1]William E. Hull, *Harbingers of Hope* (Tuscaloosa: University of Alabama Press, 2007), 127.

[2]William Wordsworth, "Ode: Intimations of Mortality from Recollections of Early Childhood," *New Oxford Book of English Verse*, 1250-1950, ed. Helen Gardner (New York: Oxford University Press, 1972), 508-513.

[3]R. Alan Culpepper, *The New Interpreter's Bible: Luke-John*, vol. 9 (Nashville: Abingdon Press, 1996), 206.

[4]Joy Barrett, writer-mentor, is the source of this version of the prayer.

[5]David Buttrick, *Homiletic: Moves and Structures* (Philadelphia: Fortress Press, 1987), 166.

[6]*The Twentieth Century Pulpit*, ed. James W. Cox (Nashville: Abingdon Press, 1978), 136.

[7]Thornton Wilder, *Our Town* (New York: Harper & Row, 1938), 45.

[8]Kenneth W. Osbeck, in *Amazing Grace: 366 Inspiring Hymn Stories for Daily Devotions* (Grand Rapids: Kregel Publications, 1990), 153, tells the following story:

George Crowly, born in Dublin, Ireland, in 1780, became an Anglican priest who ministered effectively in the slums of London. In 1854, at the age of seventy-four, Crowly published for his congregation *Psalms and Hymns for Public Worship*. Only one hymn from that collection survives: "Spirit of God, Descend Upon My Heart." We are blessed because of it. One petition of this prayer-hymn is a worthy extension of the prayer of the father of the afflicted child, who, in the valley of the Transfiguration, prayed, "I believe; help my unbelief" (Mark 9:24b).

CHAPTER 2

BEYOND GREED ...
An Inside Job

2 Kings 5:1-27

And many lepers were in Israel in the time of Elisha the prophet, and none of them was cleansed except Naaman the Syrian.
—Luke 4:27

General Naaman of the Syrian-Israeli conflict could be compared to our American General Schwarzkopf of the Gulf War: "Stormin' Norman," "Stormin' Naaman."[1]

General Naaman is a "mighty man of valor," but has one problem that renders him helpless. His "dress blues" are weighted with ribbons and stripes and medals of honor, but they hide a horrible secret: leprosy. Naaman is a mighty man of valor, but he is a leper. Only a miracle can save him.

Naaman's story is "A Tale of Two Miracles." One miracle is given in the form of a cure; the other miracle is given in the form of a curse. Both miracles pivot on "an inside job."

Miracle One: The Evangelist in the Kitchen

Employed in General Naaman's private quarters is a Jewish prisoner of war. We are not given her name, rank, or serial number. She was captured during the Syrian invasion of Israel, brought back as a slave, and forced to work in Naaman's private mess hall. The only fact we are given about her is her faith: She believes that the Hebrew prophet Elisha has the gift of healing and that the grace of the God of Israel extends to all people, regardless of race, religion, or national origin.

One day the nameless servant, awash in breakfast dishes, sighs to her mistress, "If only my master would see the prophet who is in Samaria! He would cure him of his leprosy" (2 Kings 5:3). The seed of hope is planted in the kitchen, and soon the entire chain of command is set atremble.

General Naaman orders up a column of chariots destined for Samaria, followed by a wagonload of loot that resembles a Brink's armored truck. The wagon is filled with bags of gold, bags of silver, and a wardrobe with ten outfits of designer fashion worth $80,000.[2] Naaman has something better than an HMO; he has cash! If there's a co-pay up front, he's prepared. What good is money to a man who will die without a miracle?

Besides a wagonload of loot, Naaman is armed with a diplomatic letter from Ben Hadad II, king of Syria, to be hand-delivered to King Jorham of Israel: "With this letter I am sending my servant Naaman to you so that you may cure him of his leprosy" (2 Kings 5:6b). Whereupon, the befuddled king rends his garments, a gesture in response to sacrilege. Is this a joke? Who does he think I am: a faith healer? "Am I God?" asks King Jorham. "Can I kill and bring back to life? Why does this fellow send someone to me to be cured of his leprosy?" (2 Kings 5:7b). But Elisha cuts through the diplomatic impasse: Let him come to me; walk-ins welcome; he shall know there is a prophet in Israel.

A Prescription in the Parsonage

Furiously driving his chariot like Ben Hur, Naaman's column comes to a halt in a cloud of dust at the prophet's front door. A servant (Gehazi?) appears amid all the commotion: "I'm General Naaman, supreme commander of the army of Syria. I have an appointment to see the prophet Elisha. He's expecting me."

"Oh yes, he's expecting you. But he can't see you now. However, he left you a prescription: you are to go down to the Jordan River (32 miles away), dip seven times, and you will be clean."

"What is this? Doesn't he know who I am?"

With that, "Stormin' Naaman" stalks off in a rage, muttering to himself: "Are not Abana and Pharpar, the rivers of Damascus, better than any of the waters of Israel? Couldn't I wash in them and be cleansed?" (2 Kings 5:12).

Fortunately, cooler heads on the general's staff prevail: "[Sir] If the prophet told you to do some great thing, would you not have done it? How much more, then, when he tells you, 'Wash and be cleansed'?" (2 Kings 5:13). Translated: "What have you got to lose other than your dignity and disease? Without a miracle you will die anyway."

The voice of reason finally penetrates the general's armor-plated ego. The mighty man of valor, shorn of his arrogance, turns his chariot toward the Jordan River where he dips his diseased flesh seven times. Obedient to the prophet's command, he rises to walk in newness of life: "Wash me thoroughly from my iniquity, and cleanse me from my sin. Purge me with hyssop, and I shall be clean: wash me, and I shall be whiter than snow" (Ps. 51:2, 7).

It's a Miracle!

A miracle of healing has saved an outsider, an enemy of Israel, a pagan who has worshipped strange gods. But the miracle pivots on the witness of a Jewish POW, a member of the faith community who obeyed the psalmist's injunction: "Let the redeemed of the Lord say so" (Ps. 107:2).

Historian Thomas Cahill contends that the story of our past is told in both "narratives of catastrophe" and "narratives of grace." The story of "Stormin' Naaman" is the narrative of catastrophe, the apocalypse of war that litters the landscape with human casualties. But the story of the Jewish slave is a narrative of grace. At a critical moment someone does something for someone else, speaks a word, bestows a gift, offers something beyond the requirement of circumstances. Such gift-givers are "the human hinges of history," upon whom swing an unforeseen future filled with hope.[3]

Such is the gift-giving evangelist in Naaman's kitchen.

Is There an Offering?

Meanwhile, General Naaman—like another outsider, the Samaritan Jesus cleansed of leprosy (Luke 17:11-19)—returns to Elisha to give thanks: "Now I know that there is no God in all the world except in Israel. So please accept a gift from your servant" (2 Kings 5:15). But Elisha refuses the gift with an oath: "As surely as the LORD lives, whom I serve, I will not accept a thing" (2 Kings 5:16). Why? Is not "the laborer worthy of wages"? (1 Tim. 5:18).

Perhaps Elisha, who once requested a double portion of the spirit of his mentor, Elijah (2 Kings 2:9), fears that two paltry bags of silver might compromise his spiritual gift. Elisha's scruples resemble the conscience of Sir Thomas More (1478-1535), who reminded his daughter: "When a man takes an oath, Meg, he holds himself in his hands, like water, and if he opens his fingers, he cannot hope to get himself back again."[4] A few men live by such scruples. But Gehazi, executive assistant to Elisha, is not one of them.

Miracle Two: Extortionist on the Road

Gehazi is a religious functionary, but he is not a religious man. Swearing a counter-oath, this opportunist declares, "I will run after [the general] and get something from him."

Soon, on the road to Syria and a new life, Naaman sees on the horizon a cloud of dust and a runner closing in with urgency. Alighting from his chariot, the general hastens toward the runner: Is all well? All is well.

"My master sent me to say, 'Two young men from the company of the prophets have just come to me from the hill country of Ephraim. Please give them a talent of silver and two sets of clothing'" (2 Kings 5:22). "Please," said the generous general, "take two talents of silver and the clothing."

The word is extortion. Back in his private quarters in Samaria, Gehazi hides his contraband in his closet. Two talents of silver and two changes of garments—not a bad little windfall for an afternoon's jog! And no one will ever know.

Alas, there is nothing hidden that shall not be revealed. Elisha is both charismatic and clairvoyant. He has seen the whole sordid transaction. Confronting his servant, Elisha asks: "Is this the time to take money or to accept clothes . . . ? Naaman's leprosy will cling to you and your descendants forever. Then Gehazi went from Elisha's presence and his skin was leprous—it had become as white as snow" (2 Kings 5:26-27).

The second miracle—the curse of leprosy—is the reversal of the first miracle—the cure of leprosy. Both miracles are an inside job.

Does Gehazi's punishment fit the crime? The scourge of leprosy —a death sentence for a petty theft? But what if Gehazi's greed burglarizes the precious jewel of another's soul—his faith?

General Naaman is a "mighty man of valor," but his newfound faith remains fragile. He is figuratively "a little one," a babe in matters of belief (1 Pet. 2:2). He knows that the witness of an insider has saved his life. What if he learns that the greed of another insider has ripped him off?

Offenses to fragile and immature faith are inevitable, but "woe to that man by whom the offense comes" (Matt. 18:7).

What is the difference between these two insiders, the nameless evangelist and Gehazi, the extortionist? That difference is explored in a classic play of the Yiddish theatre titled *The Dybbuk*.[5]

In this play, two young men are the best of friends. They both marry, and soon their wives are expectant mothers. The two friends swear an oath to each other that if one has a son and the other a daughter, their children will marry and their friendship will be sealed for eternity. One does have a son, the other a daughter, and their fathers betroth them to each other.

But the two friends drift apart. The one with a son becomes a scholar, as does his son after him. The other becomes a wealthy merchant and soon forgets his oath to his friend. The two young people are fated to meet and fall in love. But the wealthy father forbids the marriage, having a more prestigious groom in mind for his daughter. The scholar's son dies of a broken heart, and his ghost enters the body of his beloved. This is the dybbuk, the alien spirit of the play's title.

While the rich father is waiting for the rabbis to arrive to exorcise the alien spirit, a mysterious stranger approaches him and says, "May I ask you a question? Look out the window and tell me what you see."

The merchant prince says, "I see people."

"Now look in the mirror and tell me what you see."

"I see myself."

"Isn't that interesting," replies the stranger. "The window is glass, and the mirror is glass. But the glass in the mirror is covered with a thin coat of silver. As soon as the silver enters the glass, people stop seeing each other and can see only themselves." The merchant realizes this calamity has befallen his family because of his greed.

The house of prayer, the church of Jesus Christ, can easily become a house of mirrors, tinted with the silver coating of self-interest. Filled with Gehazi types, it may reflect the prevailing culture of greed, envy, and consumerism. When that happens to a church, people such as Robert Southey confess, "I could believe in Christ if he did not drag about behind him that leprous bride, the church."

But the house of prayer, loved by Christ and cleansed by the washing of water with the Word, offers at its best a window of worship.

Through that window, worshippers see a vision of outsiders without hope and a God whose healing grace stretches to the ends of the earth.

Both the reflection and the vision remain—an inside job.

A Prayer

Wilt Thou forgive that sin which I have won
Others to sin, and made my sin their door?
Wilt Thou forgive that sin which I did shun
A year or two, but wallowed in a score?
When Thou hast done, Thou hast not done,
For I have more.

I have a sin of fear, that when I have spun
My last thread, I shall perish on the shore;
But swear by Thyself, that at my death Thy Son
Shall shine as he shines now, and heretofore;
And having done that, Thou hast done;
I fear no more.

—John Donne[6]

Notes

[1]Robert Jacks, *Just Say the Word! Writing for the Ear* (Grand Rapids: Wm. B. Erdmans Publishing, 1996), 176.

[2]Ibid., 178.

[3]Thomas Cahill, *How the Irish Saved Civilization* (New York: Anchor Books, 1995), 100-101.

[4]Sir Thomas More, "A Man for All Seasons," www.decentfilms.com/reviews/manforallseasons.ltul.

[5]Harold S. Kushner, *Overcoming Life's Disappointments* (New York: Alfred A. Knoff, 2006), 101.

[6]According to David L. Edwards, in *John Donne: Man of Flesh and Spirit* (Grand Rapids: Wm. B. Eerdmans Publishing, 2002), 20, Anglican poet-preacher John Donne is remembered as a "Man of Flesh and Spirit." His prodigal youth prepared him for the prayer of the Psalmist: "Do not remember the sins of my youth or my transgressions; according to your lovingkindness remember me, for your goodness' sake, O Lord" (Ps. 25:7). Donne retained throughout his life "a memory of yesterday's pleasures, fear of tomorrow's dangers." But the poet's sensitivity to sin's consequences made him fear its potential injury to other persons. Thus he offered "A Prayer to the Father," in *Poems of John Donne*, vol. 1, ed. E. K. Chambers (London: Lawrence & Bullen, 1896), 213.

CHAPTER 3

BEYOND LAWLESSNESS ...
The Ten Commandments
Are Portable

Jeremiah 31:33b

In the Decalogue, a foundation is laid for the order of the community, a foundation that continues . . . for all actions on the part of God's people as they seek to live in community and order their lives.
—*Patrick D. Miller, Jr.*[1]

The American public square is now almost naked of Christian symbols, and many believers feel bereft. Among the last symbols to leave were the Ten Commandments. Film clips from a courthouse in Alabama capture the skirmish in our culture wars: armed deputies carting off the Decalogue as protestors, weeping and praying, fling themselves in the path of this latest exodus.

Many of the faithful lament their loss, for example, Mary Magdalene at the empty tomb: "They have taken away my Lord, and I know not where they have laid him" (John 20:13b). Actually, the symbols of faith, not its substance, have been taken away. While the Decalogue has disappeared, the moral law remains.

Perhaps the removal of the Commandments from the courthouse is really a parable of their centuries-long existence. They have always been portable. From the beginning, the Ten Commandments given by God to Moses, written on tablets of stone, were placed—along with Aaron's rod—in an oblong wooden box called the Ark of the Covenant. Borne on wooden poles on the shoulders of priests, the ark—much like a sacred vagabond—was carried in the vanguard of the pilgrim people.

The wooden box came to symbolize both the presence and the power of God (Exod. 25:1-22).

But God is not confined to a box, and the experience of God is not confined to a time or place. The late Carlyle Marney, a Baptist preacher and poet from the hills of east Tennessee, once labeled all religious experience as a "come-and-go affair."[2] God is like quicksilver. He never stays in one place very long. Religious experience may come to a person with shattering impact, like a hammer that splits the rock or a divine laser that emblazons truth into stone. We try to protect and preserve the experience by building a monument around it, only to learn the revelation is always a "come-and-go"—never a "come-and-stay"—affair. Religious experience must somehow become portable to remain viable.

So the traumatic disappearance of the Decalogue from the county courthouse in Alabama is simply another departure in an itinerant career that reads like a travelogue of the Holy Land:

From the smoke on Mt. Sinai where the Commandments were written in stone, to the "tent of meeting" at Shiloh (Judg. 18:31), in the days when the judges ruled . . . From the "tent of meeting" to the plains of Ashdod, where it was borne into battle only to be captured by the Philistines, who placed it in their Temple of Dagon (Judg. 16:23), only to discover their citizens plague-struck and their wooden god decapitated . . . From the temple of Dagon eventually to Solomon's temple in Jerusalem where the Ark is permanently placed (they believed!) in the Holy of Holies, accessible only to the high priest (Lev. 16:30) on the day of atonement . . . And, finally, from the Holy of Holies the Ark of the Covenant is swallowed up in Babylonian captivity (Psalm 137), never to be seen again (although the movie film character, "Indiana Jones," is still out searching for it).

One fact remains: The Ten Commandments are portable; they come and go, but the moral law remains.

Perhaps the greatest irony is not the disappearance of the Decalogue from the county courthouse, but rather its departure from the church's meeting house. The Reformers, Luther and Calvin, designated the church as the new Ark of the Covenant commissioned to house the Ten Commandments. English law decreed that the Decalogue, the Apostles Creed, and the Lord's Prayer be painted on the walls of churches and recited by the congregations every Sunday. Remnants of this law remain visible today in the architecture of Anglican churches of colonial Virginia.[3]

By the end of the twentieth century, the Decalogue had again disappeared, both from the church's architecture and the church's worship. No one seems to have noticed. Why did this happen? "The Commandments are too negative," some say. "The Commandments are inappropriate in the American cult of positive thinking," others say. "The Commandments, in a time of consumer religion, are too demanding," say others.[4] Perhaps, in further irony, the preaching of the grace of God has finally eclipsed the law of God.

Barbara Brown Taylor, the distinguished Episcopal preacher and author, studied theology at Yale. Oftentimes professors assigned term papers and placed books on related topics on reserve in the library. Invariably, the book she needed would be missing from the reserve shelf. "Is this book checked out?" Barbara once asked the librarian. "Oh, no," came the reply, "it's stolen. The divinity students are the worst in the university about stealing books." "And why is this true?" Barbara asked. "Grace!" The librarian exclaimed. "You preachers are always talking about 'grace.' Don't worry about sin. Grace will cover it. You would help us librarians if occasionally you would preach on the law of God, as in 'Thou shalt not steal!'"[5]

And so the Decalogue keeps disappearing: from the antiquity of the ancient Near East, the courthouse in Alabama, the library at Yale, and the mainline church on Main Street. The Ten Commandments are portable. They come and go, but the moral law remains.

The moral law remains because the final Ark of the Covenant is the human heart. There, the Commandments become internalized. In the worst political and theological crisis of his prophetic career, Jeremiah sees the Holy City in ruins, the temple razed, and the Ark of the Covenant with its pillars of stone swallowed up in Babylonian oblivion. But he hears the voice of God promise a new covenant and a new ark: "I will put my law in their minds and write it on their hearts. I will be their God, and they will be my people" (Jer. 31:33b).

The promise is fulfilled in the upper room, where Jesus, on the night of his betrayal, takes the cup and says to the apostles, "This cup which is poured out for you is the new covenant in my blood" (Luke 22:20b). Furthermore, instead of abolishing the Ten Commandments, Jesus adds the Eleventh Commandment: "A new commandment I give to you, that you love one another, even as I have loved you" (John 13:34).

Therefore, in the cross of Christ, and by the grace of God, the covenant people are delivered from the bondage of sin and death. We live no longer by the law, but in the law, and the law lives in us, etched in our minds and engraved in our hearts. Thus, the commandments of God are as pliable as human affection and as portable as human personality.

The promise of God to internalize the moral law is the occasion for a moral breakthrough in the faith community. Jeremiah senses that an old proverb is being discarded: "The fathers have eaten sour grapes, and the children's teeth are set on edge" (Jer. 31:29). The proverb once provided a perennial excuse for the blame game, but now the law is written on everyone's heart. Heretofore, "Each man who eats sour grapes, his teeth will be set on edge" (Jer. 31:30).

This breakthrough in personal responsibility will kindle a renewed ethical sensitivity for the moral well-being of the community.

Garrison Keillor, creator of the mythical town of Lake Wobegon in Minnesota, tells of a character in that town, Jim Nordberg, who confessed his temptation to adultery. A woman in Nordberg's office was finding him more interesting and attractive than his wife did, and the two of them planned a tryst in Chicago (so much for the Seventh Commandment!). They told their spouses the meeting was a required company seminar (so much for the Ninth Commandment!). But while waiting for the woman to pick him up, Nordberg's conscience began an unnerving conversation about personal responsibility for the moral health of the community. And Nordberg, Keillor's fictional character, began to reflect:

> As I sat on the lawn looking down the street, I saw that we all depend on each other. I saw that my sins are no more secret than an earthquake. All these houses and all these families . . . my infidelity would somehow shake them. It will pollute the drinking water. It will make noxious gases come out of the ventilators in the elementary school. When we scream in senseless anger, blocks away a little girl we do not know spills a bowl of gravy all over a white tablecloth. If I went to Chicago with this woman who is not my wife, somehow the school patrol will forget to guard the intersection and someone's child will be injured. A sixth grade teacher will

eliminate South America from geography. Our minister will decide, "I'm not going to give that sermon on the poor." . . .

Somehow my adultery will cause the man at the grocery store to say, "[who cares about] the health department? This sausage was good yesterday; there certainly can't be anything wrong with it today."[6]

Nordberg wrestled with his conscience, and both won. In refusing to commit an act our culture considers casual and consensual, Nordberg had discerned that, as Keillor says, "far from being hidden, each sin is another crack in the world."[7] For Nordberg, the Decalogue is a living document. In Lake Wobegon, the Commandments no longer hang in the halls of the courthouse, which is government property; neither are they painted on the walls of the Lutheran church where Nordberg worships. But the Commandments are written on the tablets of his mind and in the tissues of his heart. Through the cultivation of an uneasy conscience, personal responsibility won out over self-indulgence. The culture would call Nordberg a fool; God would call him free.

To be sure, the siren voices of temptation sometimes muffle the voice of conscience and consequently everybody loses. The best among us confess that the flesh is weak. In human frailty we may keep those unwise appointments in Chicago, or elsewhere, that eventually lead to disappointment and regret. But while we live in the law, and the law lives in us, we still live by grace. When the tribunal of conscience accuses, Jesus Christ—the "Decalogue Man,"[8] the Son of Law—argues our defense before the throne of grace. "In whatever our heart condemns us, God is greater than our heart, and knows all things" (1 John 3:20).

Carlyle Marney was correct: All religious experience is a "come-and-go affair." The American public square at the heart of the secular city is empty; Christian symbols have disappeared; the Ten Commandments are out of sight, but not out of mind—especially for those who cultivate the mind of Christ. The Commandments are still on the move—from Mt. Sinai to Jerusalem, from Lake Wobegon to Chicago.

But the Commandments of God remain what they have always been: portable and powerful. You can take them with you!

A Prayer

Have mercy upon me, O God, according to your loving kindness; according to the multitude of your tender mercies . . . Blot out my transgressions. Wash me thoroughly from my iniquity, and cleanse me from my sin. . . . Create in me a clean heart, O God, and renew a steadfast spirit within me. . . . O Lord, open my lips, and my mouth shall show forth your praise. For you do not desire sacrifice, or else I would give it; you do not delight in burnt offerings. The sacrifices of God are a broken spirit, a broken and contrite heart. These, O God, you will not despise.[9]

—Prayer of David following his
confession of adultery and murder
Psalm 51:1-2, 10, 15-17

Notes

[1]Patrick D. Miller, Jr. "The Place of the Decalogue in the Old Testament and Its Law," *Interpretation: A Journal of Bible and Theology* 43 (July 1989): 229.

[2]Carlyle Marney, "A Come-and-Go Affair," *The Twentieth Century Pulpit*, ed. James W. Cox (Nashville: Abingdon Press, 1978), 135.

[3]Miller, 272.

[4]Ibid., 274.

[5]Story told by Barbara Brown Taylor, in *Speaking of Sin* (Cambridge: Cowley Publications, 2001), 52.

[6]Story told by Ralph C. Wood in *Contending for the Faith: Essays in the Church's Engagement with Culture* (Waco: Baylor University Press, 2003), 151-152.

[7]Ibid.

[8]Miller, 279.

CHAPTER 4

BEYOND POLITICS ...
The King and the Knight
Have Another Move

1 Samuel 8:1-22

Politics proper always competes with religion (joining it . . . when it must, and absorbing it when it can) in order to promise if not a life beyond, then a new deal on this earth, and a leader smiling charismatically from the placards.[1]

—*Erik Erikson*[1]

The calendar declares another election year. America is again seeking a political savior. Surely, someone smiling charismatically from the placards can deliver us from our inner demons and the grip of systemic evil.

Once, in an airport coffee shop, a man was perusing the bleak headlines of the morning paper: another car bombing in Baghdad, a deranged shooter in a shopping mall. (The *New York Times* logo describes it well: "All the news that's fit to print.") The man, standing up and slapping the paper, exclaimed to no one in particular: "Anyone who can straighten out the mess we're in, we'll elect 'em God!"[2]

Indeed we will, despite the First Commandment, "You shall have no other gods before me" (Exod. 20:3).

The mood of the man in the airport matches that of the elders in Israel, who call for a referendum on God. Their words to Samuel, the judge, are cruel and confrontational: "We're in a mess. You are now a political dinosaur in a dysfunctional religious institution. Your sons are a disgrace and unworthy of your office. Now make us a king to judge us like all the nations. We'll elect him God."

Samuel is crushed and seeks the consolation of prayer. "They have not rejected you," says the Lord, "but they have rejected me, that I should not reign over them" (1 Sam. 8:7).

And when the votes are counted in the referendum at Ramah—home to Samuel—God is voted out of office. Rebecca West wisely observed that when politics comes in the door, truth flies out the window.[3] Our Scripture text from 1 Samuel 8 prompts us to ponder those conflicting voices of the political caucus.

The Voice of the People

Listen to the voice of the people. Listen to the choice of the people. "Now make us a king to judge us like all the nations" (1 Sam. 8:6). But you, Israel, are not like all the nations. "You are a royal priesthood, a holy nation, a peculiar people of God's own possession, that you may proclaim the excellencies of him who called you out of darkness into his marvelous light" (1 Pet. 2:9). But Israel wants to be like the other nations; like them in conquest, in taxation, in militarism, in power, in pride.

Strange, that a people so soon delivered by God from Egyptian slavery, through the Red Sea, across the River Jordon, into the land flowing with milk and honey—and freedom—would so soon forget the past. Strange, that a liberated people would so soon fondle a model of leadership fashioned not after Moses, but after Pharaoh.

It's ironic that the Exodus should come full circle. Moses delivers Israel from the empire of Egypt, but Solomon eventually establishes the empire of Egypt in Israel. The first step in that fatal journey is the demand of the elders: "Now make us a king to judge us like all the nations."

The choice of the people confirms one of history's lessons: Freedom is not a universal value. Power is a universal value.[4]

In the Great War of Europe, eleven million men and women perished to make the world safe for democracy. And yet, the twentieth century and the planet Earth became a theater of war in the round, dominated by tyrants whose lust for blood was exceeded only by their lust for power. The fragile flower of freedom—like gospel seed sown on stony ground—is often stomped by the marching of hob-nailed boots!

Freedom, for instance, has not flourished in the frozen vastness of Russia, although its soil has been fertilized by the blood of martyrs and saints. Rather, tyranny flourishes there.

In 2007 the editors of *Time* magazine featured on their cover Vladimir Putin, Russia's prime minister, as "Man of the Year." Putin was selected, the editors reported, for "choosing order before freedom." The story's summary, "A Tsar Is Born," signals another political reincarnation. The more things change, the more they stay the same. The editors defended their dubious distinction by voting for "achievement" instead of "character." The résumé of the "Man of the Year" is revealing: Experience—KGB, Secret Police; Religion—Agnostic; Favorite author—Machiavelli; Latest achievement—Single-handedly dismounted the machinery of democracy and freedom in Russia without firing a shot! Mr. Putin's portrait hangs in the gallery with other "achievers" including Adolph Hitler and Josef Stalin.[5]

So the elders of Israel and the editors of *Time* choose order before freedom. And we hear a chilling echo from the past: "Now make us a king to judge us like all the nations." The sacred historian believes the choice of order before freedom is a fatal attraction.

The Real King-Maker

But listen to the voice of God. Listen to the choice of God. Rising from the raucous political caucus, the choice of God breaks the political deadlock. God casts his vote with the elders and against Samuel: "Now heed their voice and make them a king" (1 Sam. 8:22a).

Author Walter Brueggemann believes the voice of God is the most interesting—and mysterious.[6] God gives permission for a king, but not approval. Is God a risk-taker? Is he like the father of a prodigal son who gives an immature boy a premature inheritance while hoping for the best, but fearing the worst? Perhaps.

But it is the Lord, not Samuel, who is the real king-maker—and king-breaker!

God practices the politics of hope. That hope is portrayed in the painting that hangs in a London gallery called *Checkmate*. The huge canvas displays a chessboard: Mephistopheles, the prince of darkness, has Faust's king in checkmate. There is no way out of perdition. But one day a grandmaster from Russia, mesmerized by the painting, suddenly breaks the silence: "It's a lie! It's a lie! The king and the knight have another move!"[7]

Chess Players
Friedrich August Moritz Retzsch, 1831
Harvard Art Museum/Fogg Museum, Gift of William Gray from the collection of
Francis Calley Gray, G3292. Photo courtesy Imaging Department © President and
Fellows of Harvard College

God is the king-maker. He always has another move. The people choose Saul of Kish as their king, a charismatic military hero who is mentally deranged and eventually self-destructs. But the Lord chooses David, a shepherd boy who becomes "a man after God's own heart" and rules a kingdom that shall not end. The king and the knight always have another move.

Once America became a house divided. The curse of slavery condemned the land. Disunion appeared the only alternative. But two fence rails symbolic of a rail splitter were brought into a political convention. A homely Lincoln was elected president, and the curse was abolished in blood. God is the king-maker!

God may lose elections, but he never loses his elect. His kingdom does not surge in the vote of a moral majority, but in the fidelity of a saving remnant. Once, the remnant got down to one man. The Roman governor, Pontius Pilate, called for a referendum on the Son of God who is labeled King of the Jews.

"Behold . . . Your King!"

The people shout, "Away with him! Away with him! Crucify him!" Pilate protests, "Shall I crucify your king?" The leaders respond, "We have no king but Caesar!" (John 19:4c-15). *Déjà vu.* Now, make us a king to judge us like all the nations. We'll elect Caesar our god. "Imperious Caesar, dead and turned to clay, might stop a hole to keep the wind away."[8]

And Jesus "suffered under Pontius Pilate . . . dead . . . buried." But the king and the knight have another move, "He is not here; he is risen!" (Matt. 28:6a).

Already, the kingdoms of this world are becoming the kingdom of our Lord and of his Christ (Rev. 11:15b). The dominoes of dominion and oppression are toppling.

A Texas evangelist in 1968 conducted a preaching mission to the underground church in Cuba. His hosts recruited a young intellectual to translate. She was a skilled linguist but a devout Marxist. She reported the preacher's every move to Castro, but translated his message flawlessly. So the preacher on the last night, looking into the faces of an oppressed people, quoted the story of the *Checkmate* painting: "Don't lose heart; don't give up hope. Remember: the king and the knight have another move." Suddenly, the translator stopped translating. The people were watching her and not the preacher, waving handkerchiefs and saying "Go ahead, baby. Go ahead, baby." She had stopped translating and started praising Jesus because she had dramatically been converted! Back home, the preacher received a letter from the translator. She was familiar with the painting in London; she, too, had lost hope in a political ideology that failed, but she recovered hope in God when she discovered that the king always has another move.[9]

Listen to the voice of God. He speaks the politics of hope. Even on Broadway the song is heard: "I'm struck like a dope with a thing called hope . . . and I can't get it out of my mind."[10]

So, the calendar declares another election year. America searches for a political savior. We are in a mess. We live in a national house divided; we wage an uncivil war. But God is somewhere in the mess, concerned not only about saving souls, but also about saving communities.

We have a king who is not Caesar. And hope is invested not in the body-politic, but in the politics of prayer.

Yet, let us be careful what we pray for. Let us always pray for discernment, for insight. The plea for discernment kindles hope and quickens accountability.

In life we don't always get what we want. But in politics? We usually get what we deserve!

A Prayer

> Look with mercy, our Father, upon this company of your people, united in worship and in this desire to know your will. Strengthen our faith so that, though we are perplexed, we may not be perplexed unto despair. Unite us in spirit with the company of your people everywhere so that, by your grace, we may be a strong fortress of faith against unbelief, of courage against faintheartedness, of the knowledge of the true God against idolatry of all who worship race, ruler, and nation or any other majesty. O God, whose service is perfect freedom, may your children be freed from the bondage of the world because they submit themselves in bondage to you. Amen.
>
> —Reinhold Niebuhr[11]

Notes

[1]Quoted by Eugene H. Peterson, in *Reversed Thunder: The Revelation of John and the Praying Imagination* (San Francisco: HarperCollins Publishers, 1991), 117.

[2]David Buttrick, *Preaching Jesus Christ: An Exercise in Homiletic Theology* (Philadelphia: Fortress Press, 1988), 47.

[3]Gordon S. Wood, *The Purpose of the Past: Reflections on the Uses of History* (New York: Penguin Press, 2008), 308.

[4]J. Rufus Fears, "The Wisdom of History," lecture (Chantilly, VA: The Teaching Company, 2007).

[5]Adi Ignatius, 19 December 2007, www.time.com/time/specials/2007/article/0,28804,1690753_1690757_1690766,00.html.

[6]Walter Brueggemann, *First and Second Samuel*, Interpretation: A Bible Commentary for Teaching and Preaching (Louisville: John Knox Press, 1990), 66.

[7]Paul Scott Wilson, *The Four Pages of the Sermon: A Guide to Biblical Preaching* (Nashville: Abingdon Press, 1999), 225.

[8]William Shakespeare, *Hamlet*, act 5, scene 1.

[9]Wilson, 225.

[10]From the musical *South Pacific*, 1945, quoted by Joy Durham Barrett.

[11]Reinhold Niebuhr, *Justice and Mercy*, ed. Ursula M. Niebuhr (New York: Harper & Row, 1974), 113.

CHAPTER 5

BEYOND COLDNESS ...
What's New about the New Commandment?

John 13:31-35

A new commandment I give to you, that you love one another, even as I have loved you, that you also love one another. By this all men will know that you are my disciples, if you have love for one another.
—John 13:34-35 (NASB)

Since moving to the mountains of North Georgia, I've been listening more and talking less—to the delight of everyone! Lately, in the silences I have heard an accent. I wonder if you are hearing it, too. At first this accent was faint, barely audible. But recently, it's becoming increasingly persistent, like the "Ping! Ping! Ping!" of a piano tuner, until finally it grates on your nerves. This accent is on the absence of God. There's a touch of melancholy about this silence, like letters delivered by the postman addressed to someone who left the house long ago with no forwarding address.[1] The absence of God is palpable to many, and some are sad.

A growing number of our more articulate voices have picked up this accent on God's absence. Recently, Larry King of CNN, who interviews the rich and famous, gave an interview himself to *Newsweek* magazine. His religion? Raised in the Jewish tradition, married to a beautiful young woman of the Mormon persuasion, he said, "I've looked out across the world for a long time now for some sign of God, only to reluctantly conclude there's nobody there."

To be sure, the experience of the absence of God is not unfamiliar, even to the faithful. Veterans of belief refer to "the cry of absence."[2] Prayer becomes a plaintive, "Dear God, where are you?"

At the Last Supper of Christ and the apostles, the cry of absence fills the upper room with alarm. The atmosphere is toxic with betrayal. Judas Iscariot rises from the table with the bread crumbs of Holy Communion still clinging to his clothing, and goes out into the night to consummate his perfidy. Whereupon, the Master, in the most tender words, declares another departure—his own: "Little children, where I am going you cannot come" (John 13:33b).

Cries of anxiety about his absence fill the room: "Lord, where are you going?" "Can I come, too?" "What will become of us?"

In response, Jesus announces a new commandment to assuage their alarm: "Love one another, even as I have loved you" (John 13:34b).

But how can this new commandment of love possibly fill the void left by the absence of Christ? The question clamors for a Christian response.

What's New about an Old Commandment?

But first, a more immediate question: What is new about the commandment of love? After all, the first and great commandment of love leaps across the centuries to Moses, who commands the people: "You shall love the Lord your God with all your heart, with all your soul, and with all your strength" (Deut. 6:5). Furthermore, "You shall love your neighbor as yourself" (Lev. 19:18).

On these two great pillars of revelation hang the law and the prophets of Judaism. What could possibly be added to ancient commandments centuries old? Just this: new people; men and women "in Christ" for whom all things have become new; men and women who are chosen by God for obedience. "You have not chosen me," says Jesus to the disciples, "but I have chosen you" (John 15:16a).

In the Old Covenant, Moses gives the Ten Commandments at Mount Sinai written on the tablets of stone. Obedience to the Ten Commandments identifies the Jewish nation as the chosen people of God. "By this all men will know you are my disciples, if you love one another" (John 13:35).

A New Ice Age?

Today, some scientists are warning us that our planet is imperiled by the process of global warming. Time will tell. But others believe our most imminent danger is not global warming, but rather the descent of a new ice age that threatens to encase the earth in hate. But God has planned a way out, and this is absolutely critical: Obedience to the new commandment of love will prevent God's chosen people from becoming the frozen people.

Prophets and poets with their sensitive antennae pick up signals long before the rest of us. As long ago as 1920, Robert Frost, America's "cracker barrel poet," foresaw the encroachment of this chilling calamity. He held with traditionalists that the world will eventually end in some apocalyptic firestorm. But if it had to perish twice, Frost concluded, "I know enough of hate / To say that for destruction ice / Is also great and would suffice."[3]

Does anyone doubt that the ice age of hate is here? Long before Robert Frost, Jesus Christ—from the vantage point of the Mount of Olives—foresaw an age of lawlessness in which "the love of most people will grow cold" (Matt. 24:12). That prophecy appears palpably fulfilled. The ice age with its rage has arrived. A bitter observer of life concluded that the line between love and hate is as sharp as a razor's edge.[4] That razor's edge cuts through every human heart, every marriage, and every congregation.

"To the angel of the church in Ephesus," writes the Spirit, "I have this . . . against you, that you have left your first love" (Rev. 2:1, 4). This once great church will soon succumb to the ice age. Apparently, this church's intense commitment to doctrinal fidelity distracted it from love's supremacy. It kept the Ten Commandments, but forgot the Eleventh: Love one another. It's tragic when the chosen people become the frozen people.

The Cardiac Principle

The emotional symptoms of the ice age of hate are demonstrable: feelings become frozen; hearts become hardened. The apostolic admonition, "Be angry, and yet do not sin; do not let the sun go down on your anger" (Eph. 4:26), is diagnostic but difficult. Too many sunsets on uncomposed quarrels will turn anger into hate.

Toni Morrison in her novel, *Beloved*, probes the residue of hate deposited by centuries of American slavery. Beloved is the mysterious figure who conceals the lost identity of some sixty million forgotten folk. The wound on the collective soul is calcified. Morrison's heroine, Sethe, says to Paul D.: "The trouble with you is, you've got a tobacco tin lodged in your chest where a big red heart used to be—its lid rusted shut."[5] What can be done with folks with such interior wounds whose feelings have distilled into rust? And yet, "Beloved" practices the "cardiac principle." She seeks to open the sluices of the human heart until the juices of feelings and affection flow freely once more.

When you think about it, that word beloved hangs as a banner over the entire Gospel of John: the beloved God who loves the world, the beloved Son who loves his own, the beloved community whose members love one another and thus practice the cardiac principle. Our own Fanny Crosby, a product of the cruel age of Toni Morrison's *Beloved*, saw the human heart not as a tobacco tin filled with rust, but as an old piano with broken keys, the symbolism expressed in her hymn, "Rescue the Perishing":

> Down in the human heart,
> Crushed by the tempter,
> Feelings lie buried that grace can restore;
> Touched by a loving heart,
> Wakened by kindness,
> Chords that are broken will vibrate once more.

Therefore, what is new about those ancient commands to love God and love one another? New people: those chosen by Christ who remain obedient to the heavenly vision (Acts 26:19).

Jesus Commands Love

The larger question remains: How does the eleventh commandment of love compensate for the absence of the historic Jesus? When the disciples of Jesus love one another as Jesus loves, then the community at large will not become bereft of Jesus. Although Christ is forever absent from the days of his flesh, he becomes at times strangely present during the days of our flesh. This fellowship often brings a greater perspective on Christ that was not apparent then. The Epistle of John wraps this reality in a golden text: "No one has beheld God at any time; if we love one another, God abides in us and his love is perfected in us" (1 John 4:12).

Even when two or three disciples of Jesus assemble in the name of Jesus, their company is enlarged by the person of Jesus, and that company has the power to transcend barriers and boundaries.

For a year and a half, our daughter, Ruth, journeyed through a long, dark valley of affliction and rehabilitation. While driving home from work in northern Virginia, Ruth's car was struck by a fence company truck driven by a young Latino man with no driver's license and who was in the country illegally. He fled to escape police charges. Ruth struggled against feelings of hate kindled by those who act irresponsibly and inflict lasting injury.

But one autumn, Ruth reported a mitigating experience: "We had our kitchen redone," she said, "and two young Latino men worked in the house all week. On Friday, one of the men walked past the bookshelves and saw the *Interpreter's Bible* commentary. He looked at me and asked, 'Are you a believer?'"

"Yes, I am," she responded.

"Said he, "I, too am a believer.""

They talked about their faith and finally the young man said, "I see you walk with a cane. I feel strongly impressed to pray for your healing. Would your husband come downstairs and join us for prayer?"

The four of them joined hands as the young Latino man in good English prayed for our daughter's healing. A friendship was formed that endures to this day. These four young adults, diverse in affluence, geography, and nationality had but one fact in common: They were disciples of Jesus, who obeyed the commandment of Jesus to "love one another."

Indeed, "Where two or three have gathered together in my name, there I am in their midst" (Matt. 18:20).

When the Lord left the earth, he gave but one command: Love one another. It is said that you cannot command love, but Jesus did. And the commandment of love is not really a burden; it is a gift. And somehow the giver appears when his love is practiced.

And who knows, maybe the Larry Kings of the community might take another look for God, not when the gospel of Jesus becomes more credible, but when disciples of Jesus become more lovable.

A Prayer

> O thou who are light to all that loves and fire to all that
> hates, let thy glory shine upon us so that love in us may
> come to life and all our hatred be consumed. . . . Come
> then again to our hearts; shine upon us in all thy fair-
> ness; burn thyself ineffaceably within; heal us, though
> by pain; save us, though by death. Amen.
>
> —W. E. Orchard[6]

Notes

[1]Philip Larkin, English poet, makes similar images of nostalgia in *Collected Poems* (New York: Farrar, Straus, and Giroux and the Marvel Press, 1993), 231.

[2]Martin E. Marty, *A Cry of Absence: Reflections for the Winter of the Heart* (San Francisco: HarperCollins, 2009), 17-18. Marty chronicles his own crisis in Chicago, which occurred in winter during his wife's battle with cancer.

[3]Robert Frost, "Fire and Ice," www.poemhunter.com/poem/fire-and-ice.

[4]W. Somerset Maugham, *The Razor's Edge* (London: Heinemann, 1944).

[5]Toni Morrison, *Beloved* (New York: Penguin Press, 1987), 116.

[6]W. E. Orchard, *The Temple* (New York: E. P. Dutton & Co., 1918), 82.

CHAPTER 6

BEYOND WORLDLINESS ...
The Highway Through Death Valley

Isaiah 40:3-8

The desert shall rejoice and blossom as the rose; . . . for waters shall burst forth in the wilderness . . .

—Isaiah 35:1, 6

During the summer of 2005 a great revival meeting broke out in Death Valley, California. The revival was wrought not by worship, but by weather. California weather is weird. For days unforeseen rains fell on Death Valley, fulfilling biblical prophecy. Suddenly, the lilies-of-the-valley perked up and put on a floor show for the bright and morning star. Roses of Sharon formed a gigantic bouquet, filling the desert with a sweet-smelling fragrance. For a moment in time, Death Valley was filled with life. Tourism exploded. Campers and SUVs clogged the roads. Park rangers, like pied pipers, led tourists across verdant hillsides, lecturing on flowers and foliage no one knew existed before the rains fell.[1]

What was happening here? The "showers of blessing" were some of those biblical "seasons of refreshing," momentarily reviving both nature and human nature. Such seasons of refreshing, sent from God, are forecasts of the future for the people of God.

More than 500 years before Christ, an unknown poet-prophet dubbed "the prophet of exile" rekindled hope in the hearts of the Hebrew people, swallowed up in Babylonian captivity.

The prophet's message reminds me of Yogi Berra. Yogi would rearrange the English language to suit himself. Once, he hurried off to speak at the Yankees' banquet at the end of the baseball season. "Yogi," someone asked, "what are you going to talk about?" "Oh," he replied, "I'm just going to reminisce about the future."

It appears appropriate in this hour—with great gratitude for all that has been—that we reminisce about the future. But before we can get to that future, we have to go through Death Valley.

The Barren Desert

Let us face a somber fact: In the prophetic consciousness, the barren desert symbolizes human life without God. The godless life is a dry and thirsty land where there is no water. This spiritual condition has evoked some of the most beautiful poetry ever wrung from the anguish of the human heart. The poet-prophet of the exile remembers his call from God: "A voice said, 'Preach.' What shall I preach? All flesh is grass. And all its beauty is the flower of the field. The grass withers, the flower fades because the breath of the Lord blows upon it. Surely the people are grass" (Isa. 40:6-7). Human life with all its spectacular beauty is beset with brevity—and vanity.

In his greatest poem, "The Wasteland," T. S. Eliot explored not a place on the map, but the landscape of his own soul. With his marriage disintegrating, his mental sanity at risk, Eliot wrote of broken images mocked by the merciless sun, dead trees without one leaf of shelter, dry stones that conceal no sound of water. He wrote confessionally toward the end of the poem: "These fragments I have shored against my ruins."[2]

Who among us has not explored that desolate landscape of troubled introspection? The poets and prophets, both ancient and modern, portray the barren desert as a dreary existence without the consolations of God.

The Spirit of Babylon Is Alive and Well

From the forlorn desert, two great building projects have arisen: men have built a great city and a tower that reaches the heavens. The name of that city? Babylon. You remember the old story from Genesis on the plains of Shinar, by the banks of the Euphrates River, beside which American Bradley tanks now patrol, the builders once gathered: "Then they said, 'Come, let us build ourselves a city, And a tower whose top is the heavens: Let us make a name for ourselves'" (Gen. 11:4).

Do you hear in those words the echo of a former boast from the Garden of Eden: "We shall be as gods"? Babylon, with its gleaming towers and hanging gardens, one of the world's ancient wonders, is a monument to human pride and arrogance. Therefore, the Bible holds Babylon in contempt. In the Old Testament, Babylon is the atheist. In the New Testament, Babylon is the antichrist. The Revelation labels Babylon "the mother of harlots" (Rev. 17:5). Because of Babylon's godless arrogance, God curses the city with the commotion of sounds, the cacophony of confusion.

Sir George Adam Smith of Aberdeen, notable scholar of Hebrew prophecy, once observed that the great hours in the history of a great city occur when it speaks through one voice.[3] Once, all of Athens spoke through the voice of Demosthenes as he rocked the cradle of democracy. Once, all of Rome spoke through the voice of Cicero as he persuaded the Senate to be a nation of laws and not of men. Once, all of Florence spoke through the voice of Savonarola as he stood in the city square with an open Bible and a thousand hearts were strangely warmed. Indeed, the great hours in the history of a great city occur when the city speaks through one voice.

But Babylon? What sounds do you hear from Babylon in the nightly news? A bedlam of conflicting rages. A medley of ancient hatreds. For the sake of our troops at risk in Babylon, we wish that city could find one voice—the voice of democracy, the voice of reason. But the ancient curse of confusion is hard to cancel.

Why bring this up? Because, while the city of Babylon lies dead and buried in the dustbin of the past, the spirit of Babylon is alive and well here in the present. Its infectious arrogance has spread from East to West. Before the end of the apostolic era, the Babylonian virus had mutated in Rome. At the end of his first epistle, written to Christians scattered across the empire, the apostle Peter penned these words: "She who is in Babylon sends greetings" (1 Pet. 5:13). The toxic spirit of Babylon can poison any city or community—or church.

Is America now a hostage held in Babylonian captivity? The late Pope John Paul once labeled the American way of life as "the culture of death."[4] Once, America was known as a "city set on a hill," giving light to the nations. But no longer. By the end of the twentieth century, the foremost symbol of America had become not a city set on a hill, but a city built in the desert: "Viva Las Vegas!" . . . playground of pleasure. It is unfortunate that a city in the desert is a symbol by which others judge us, especially our enemies.

But the more pressing question arises: Has the Babylonian spirit infected the church? It is one thing when the church is in Babylon; it is another when Babylon is in the church.

On Ash Wednesday our church observed the solemn service of the imposition of the ashes on the brow and the declaration of the liturgy, "You are dust, and to dust you shall return." We were filing toward the Remembrance Table when I saw a young woman wearing a T-shirt bearing a bold message: "What happens in Vegas stays in Vegas."

What mixed messages are signaled even from the church's altar. One message says, "Life is a battleground; you are mortal." Another says, "Life is a playground; you are not accountable." We cannot keep the church out of Babylon; to keep Babylon out of the church will present a critical challenge.

The Highway of Holiness

While men have built a city in the desert, God has built a highway through the desert—"the highway of holiness," "the roadway of the redeemed," "the highway of our God." All eyes searched the highway for the sign of someone who has promised to appear. Handel's music has kept the prophet's promise alive: "And the glory of the Lord shall be revealed, And all flesh shall see it together." And again, from Handel: "Say to the cities of Judah, Behold your God."

These prophecies were partially fulfilled in the words of Pontius Pilate on Good Friday. Parading the Christ before the mob, he shouted: "*Ecce Homo!*" (Behold, the Man!). Today, in the old city of Jerusalem spans the "*Ecce Homo* Arch" overlooking the Via Dolorosa, the way of the cross, the highway of our God. That highway will take you home!

The days of the Lord's flesh have been defined as "Jesus on the road with his friends, looking for more friends." These friends of Jesus are called "God's graduates." We hear it from Jesus himself: "No longer do I call you servants . . . But I have called you friends," for "all things that I heard from my Father I have made known to you" (John 15:15).

For more than a century, Jesus has found in this fellowship more friends who walked with him the narrow way that leads to life. I see some of their faces in memory, beyond our reach but not our affection. Today, he still whispers: "Follow me."

Journeying with him on the highway to holiness will require from us perhaps a mid-course correction, or even a radical change of direction—in a word, "repentance."

In the 1950s at the First Baptist Church of Gainesville, Georgia, there served a beloved pastor, Franklin Owen. In his book, *Slightly Soiled Saints,*[5] he told the following story.

One year in June he flew to San Francisco, checked into the Saint Francis Hotel, and attended the Southern Baptist Convention. But the day before his return, he lost his plane ticket. He stopped at the travel desk in the lobby and explained his loss to the ticket agent.

She said, "You'll have to take the train back to Atlanta."

"Goodness," he complained, "that will take more than two days!"

At that moment, Dr. Forrest Lanier, pastor of the First Baptist Church of Rome, Georgia, appeared and said, "Frank, what's going on?"

"Oh, Forrest," said Dr. Owen, "I've lost my plane ticket. I'll have to ride the train back to Atlanta."

"Frank," replied Dr. Lanier. "Why are we in such a hurry? You and I have been friends for years. When have we ever caught up on our visiting? You know what? I'm going to ride the train back with you."

Dr. Lanier turned in his ticket to the agent. "Ma'am, please cancel my flight on #651 tomorrow and put me on the train with my friend."

The following day's journey was one of leisure, filled with beautiful western scenery. The two ministers talked and laughed—and prayed. But at the end of the first day, as the train pulled through a junction, a bundle of newspapers of *The San Francisco Chronicle* was tossed on board, bearing the ominous headline:

FLIGHT #651 CRASHES: NO SURVIVORS!

"Frank," said Dr. Lanier, "thank God for your friendship. Were it not for our friendship, tonight my wife would be a widow and the pulpit in Rome would be vacant."

Thank God for Christ's transforming friendship. To walk with him requires of us, as it did for Forrest Lanier, a change of direction, a turning and returning. Jesus said that the victims of falling towers—and aircraft—are no more morally guilty than those who escape them.

Rather, the calamities of nature—and human nature—are a summons to repentance and a change of direction.

To be sure, the journey with Christ is a perilous one. Ours is a world in which sparrows fall to the earth and men go down in flames. But underneath are the "everlasting arms." They hold us securely in his love until we reach the New Jerusalem, where sorrow and sighing shall flee away.

A Prayer

> Gracious Father, we pray for the holy catholic church. Fill it with all truth, in all truth with all peace; where it is corrupt, purify it; where it is in error, direct it; wherein anything is amiss, reform it. Where it is right, strengthen it; where it is in want, provide for it; where it is divided, reunite it; for the sake of Jesus Christ thy Son our Savior. Amen.[6]
>
> —*The Book of Common Prayer*

Notes

[1]Brian Williams of NBC News devoted nine minutes to this event in *Death Valley*.

[2]Carol Seymour-Jones, *Painted Shadow: A Life of Vivienne Eliot* (New York: Doubleday, 2001), 297.

[3]George Adam Smith, *The Book of Isaiah*, vol. 2 (New York: Harper & Brothers Publishers, 1899), 208.

[4]Donald De Marco and Benjamin Wiker, *Architects of the Culture of Death* (San Francisco: Ignatius Press, 2004), 378.

[5]Franklin Owen, *Slightly Soiled Saints* (Williamsburg, KY: Cumberland College, 1985), 81.

CHAPTER 7

BEYOND EXHAUSTION ...
The World Is a Waiting Room

Isaiah 40:27-31

Why do you say, O Jacob, and speak, O Israel: "My way is hidden from the LORD, *and my just claim is passed over by my God"? Have you not known? Have you not heard? The everlasting God, the* LORD, *the Creator of the ends of the earth, neither faints nor is weary. His understanding is unsearchable. He gives power to the weak, and to those who have no might he increases strength. Even the youths shall faint and be weary, and the young men shall utterly fall, but those who wait on the* LORD *shall renew their strength; they shall mount up with wings like eagles, they shall run and not be weary, they shall walk and not faint.*

—Isaiah 40:27-31

"All the world's a stage," declared our greatest dramatist, "and all the men and women merely players; they have their exits and their entrances."[1] Shakespeare meant that even the most brilliant plays portrayed in London's Globe Theater pale in comparison with the comedies and tragedies played out on London's streets. Truth is stranger than fiction—and far more interesting to those with eyes to see and ears to hear.

A Waiting Room: Allegory of Life—and Death

If all the world's a stage, then every waiting room is a little theater. Waiting is probably the most wearisome and worrisome time we shall ever spend. Human inventions to pass the time are endlessly creative, and yet contradictory—considering that we have so little time. Some ask, "Are we amusing ourselves to death?"[2] Probably.

In a large surgical waiting room in a hospital in Atlanta, men and women waited—some for hours—for a surgeon to appear and report on a loved one's procedure. A "pink lady" sat at a desk staring at a red telephone connected with the operating room. The digital sweep of the red secondhand on the huge wall clock signaled to some people that today might be their longest day. A few feet down the hallway a Starbucks was thriving, its aroma wafting up the staircase. The oblong waiting room resembled the midway at the county fair with several venues in which mini-dramas played out before the steady stream of passers-by.

In the center of the room in a cluster of chairs sat some fifteen members of an extended family. Their attention was riveted on the antics of a two-year-old toddler. They tossed the toddler up and down and back and forth to each member, who in turn made Halloween faces and romper room sounds that kept the child laughing. The novelty of a new baby made that family oblivious to the passing of time. Scripture was fulfilled: "A little child shall lead them" (Isa. 11:6).

Nearby, a grandmother sat at a card table with a deck of cards and two sleep-deprived grandsons. Grandma shuffled and dealt the cards with the skills of a blackjack dealer in a coastal casino. She kept score on a pad and was obviously winning. But the body language of the boys protested: "We don't want to play cards. We don't even want to be here. Why don't you let us sleep?" Indeed, "even the youths shall faint and grow weary, and the young men shall utterly fall" (Isa. 40:30).

But in a deserted corner of the room, two women sat face-to-face and talked intensely—and tearfully. One was the hospital chaplain who had been summoned by the pink lady; the other was presumably the wife of a patient whose surgeon had reported ominous and frightening complications—as in cardiac arrest, life support, ICU. She was assured that everything possible was being done, that family members should be notified, and that the next twenty-four hours were absolutely critical. Therefore the two women began their vigil with joined hands and heads bowed as muffled prayers poured through the sound of sobs.

Different people wait differently. Some, with nothing to lose, spend the time of waiting at play. Others, with everything to lose, spend the time of waiting in prayer. Those who play become exhausted; those who pray become energized. As the waiting room finally emptied, the two card-playing teenagers were straddled across lounging chairs utterly spent. But the prayerful young woman, having dabbed her eyes with tissue and applied fresh make-up, stood up straight, put on her coat, and embraced the chaplain. Then she walked toward the exit, her face resolutely fixed toward the future as Christ had set his face toward Jerusalem. During one surgical shift a divine promise had been fulfilled: "They that wait upon the Lord shall renew their strength" (Isa. 40:31).

A Three-Fold Surge of Strength

Those who wait on the Lord are promised a three-fold surge of strength: They shall soar like an eagle. They shall run like an Olympian. They shall walk like a pedestrian. Ecstasy to soar, energy to run, endurance to walk . . . these three, and the greatest of these is the strength to walk and not faint.

Biblical scholar Sir George Adam Smith[3] concluded that soaring and running are less difficult than the steady pace demanded by "the humdrum dullness of ordinary days."[4] The capacity to walk is the final test of biblical faith.[5] The greatest confessions of faith are not uttered by learned men in committee, but by trudging souls in the valley who shout to curious onlookers: "I'm still on my feet!" After all, long after the marathons of speed are forgotten, the walk-a-thons of endurance are remembered.

Americans still recall that overland traveler who walked all the way from San Francisco to New York. He said the hardest obstacles were neither the Rockies nor the Alleghenies; his greatest perils were not the swollen Mississippi nor the turbulent Ohio. What almost defeated him was the sand in his shoes![6] But he kept walking.

Similarly, the prophet portrays the energized believer in exile who walks the 1,200-mile trek from Babylon to Jerusalem. Beginning by the banks of the Euphrates River, the exile trudges up the ancient trade route that becomes "the way of the Lord" and eventually down the Syrian desert that is "a highway for our God"—where "every valley [is] exalted and every mountain and hill brought low, the crooked made straight and the rough places smooth" (Isa. 40:3-5)—until he finally crosses the River Jordan and ascends to the Mount of Olives, surrounded by the hills of Zion and the ruins of Jerusalem. "And the glory of the Lord shall be revealed, and all flesh shall see it together" (Isa. 40:5).

The World Is a Waiting Room

The phrase, "all flesh," moves the promise of God from the particular to the universal. Did not Kierkegaard, the Dane, infer that if he asked the philosopher Hegel for directions to a street address in Copenhagen, Hegel would hand him a map of Europe where Denmark would be no larger than a steel pinpoint?[7]

Like the philosopher Hegel, the prophet of the exile has moved a particular promise of God (strength to walk) made to a particular people (a remnant of Jews) at a particular place (by the rivers of Babylon) to a universal inclusion that encircles the centuries and encompasses the ends of the earth.

Simultaneous to the waiting young woman in the hospital in Atlanta, there appeared a Fox News broadcast from Iraq of a sixteen-year-old Arab girl in a field hospital in Baghdad. The camera told her story in three poignant scenes:

In scene one, she lies on a bed covered with a smock, after both her legs were blown off at the knees when she stepped on an IED (improvised explosive device). Her deep brown eyes resemble a frightened deer paralyzed by a beam of light.

In scene two, an American Army orthopedic surgeon stands beside her bed holding up her x-rays. "You will walk again, I promise," says he. Her eyes suddenly brighten with a ray of hope.

Scene three is in rehab where she "solos" beyond the hand rails and pivots on her prostheses toward the audience of doctors, nurses, and patients who are cheering loudly and shouting. "Look at her! She's walking. She's walking."

A promise made 2,500 years ago by the God of Abraham, Isaac, and Jacob to a remnant of Jews is fulfilled in the life of an Arab teenager through the skills of an American surgeon. God's promise of strength, once no larger than a steel pinpoint, has encircled the earth and penetrated all cultures.

The Lord Is Waiting To Be Gracious

Therefore, to wait on the Lord is the antidote to despair. "Wait on the Lord: Be of good courage, and he shall strengthen your hearts. Wait, I say, on the Lord" (Ps. 27:14).

When you wait on the Lord, you will discover that he, too, is waiting—patiently and undiscouraged. The Lord does not grow weary in waiting; his patience is not penetrated by petulance: "With the Lord one day is as a thousand years, and a thousand years as one day" (2 Pet. 3:8). But the Lord knows there is something in you and me that makes the waiting necessary. Is it fear? Is it unbelief? When we begin to seriously confront that "something"—whatever it is—the time of waiting will be over.

A veteran missionary to China on furlough in Hawaii confessed to a friend that he knew the question God would ask him on the day of judgment: "Why didn't you let me bless you more?" When challenged for biblical support, he turned in his Chinese Bible to Isaiah's prophecy: "The Lord is waiting to be gracious to you" (Isa. 30:18).[8]

The Lord is waiting to be gracious to you and me. I do not know the question on the final exam, but of one fact I am sure: When you wait on the Lord, you will discover that all the time the Lord has been waiting on you.[9]

A Prayer

> Almighty God, in whose eternity our transient lives are held, whose will is our peace, who has come among us in great humility, make us wise to wait for Thee, to wish for Thee, to watch for Thee until the breaking of the day. Through Jesus Christ our Lord, Amen.
>
> —George A. Buttrick[10]

Notes

[1]William Shakespeare, *As You Like It*, act 2, scene 7.

[2]Neil Postman, *Amusing Ourselves to Death* (New York: Penguin Books, 2006), 156-157.

[3]James D. Smart, *History and Theology in Second Isaiah: A Commentary on Isaiah 35, 40-66* (Philadelphia: Westminster Press, 1965), 63.

[4]James Leo Green, *God Reigns* (Nashville: Broadman Press, 1968), 127.

[5]Smart, 63.

[6]Paul Scherer, *The Place Where Thou Standest* (New York: Harper & Brothers Publishers, 1942), 151.

[7]George Arthur Buttrick, *God, Pain, and Evil* (Nashville: Abingdon Press, 1966), 118.

[8]Related by Carl Bates, while pastor of First Baptist Church, Charlotte, North Carolina, in a sermon titled, "Why Didn't You Let Me Bless You More?"

[9]Marvin Tate, professor of Old Testament interpretation of the Southern Baptist Theological Seminary, Louisville, Kentucky, often used this expression in his exposition of the Isaiah passage.

[10]George Buttrick, *Pulpit Digest*, vol. 71, no. 481 (September/October 1986): 378. Dr. Buttrick, famed Presbyterian pastor and preacher to Harvard University, taught his theology students that the thoughtful preparation of the pastoral prayer was even more important than the preparation of the sermon.

CHAPTER 8

BEYOND INSIGNIFICANCE ...
It's a Wonderful Life

John 15:22-25

If I had not come and spoken to them, they would have no sin, but now they have no excuse for their sin.

—*John 15:22* [1]

When Jimmy Stewart died at his Hollywood home, the next day headlines carried his epitaph: "A Wonderful Life."

Jimmy Stewart of Hollywood will always be remembered as George Bailey of Bedford Falls in Frank Capra's film (1946), *It's a Wonderful Life*. The movie, watched by millions during the Christmas season, addresses the universal question, "What is a life that matters?" [1]

Ironically, George Bailey wants to be Jimmy Stewart. He dreams of leaving Bedford Falls, joining the military service in World War II, flying a B-17 bomber, and returning home a hero. But his father's sudden death leaves George to run the family building and loan business. The town depends on his integrity.

The story pivots on a mistake made by a beloved employee that threatens to bankrupt the business and deliver the town into the greedy hands of the villain, Mr. Potter.

Driven by desperation, George staggers through a snowstorm to the bridge over the river from which he will end his life. He mutters: "I'm a failure. My life doesn't matter. I'll never be missed."

But on the bridge George encounters his guardian angel, whose mission is to convince George he is not a failure and that his life still matters. In a series of flashbacks the guardian angel parallels the life of George Bailey with the history of Bedford Falls. The results are demonstrable: If George Bailey had not lived, Bedford Falls would have become "Pottersville"—a town without spirit, without hope, and most of all, without love.[2]

It's a wonderful life because it's a life that matters.

What If …

John's Gospel asks us to ponder a far more appalling possibility: What if Jesus Christ had not been born? What if the angel Gabriel had not persuaded Mary to journey to Bethlehem and deliver her baby? Without that one solitary life, Planet Earth would have become "Pottersville"— a cosmic dump.

What if Christ had not come and spoken words of eternal life? Our Bible would end with the prophecy of Malachi unfulfilled. The twenty-seven books of our New Testament would not exist. Classics of inspiration, such as *The Imitation of Christ* and *Pilgrim's Progress*, would not have been conceived. Familiar sounds of "The Hallelujah Chorus" and "Amazing Grace" would not have been heard.

Can you imagine a funeral service without the comfort of John 14:1? "Let not your hearts be troubled; believe in God, believe also in me."

What if Christ had not come and done the works that no one else could do? Only he has the authority to build his church imbued with the power to storm the gates of hell (Matthew 16). What if this meeting-house in which we have met for worship—whose cornerstone declares, "The church's one foundation is Jesus Christ her Lord"—did not exist? Today, this property might be a gambling casino or a pagan temple housing ancient gods made of wood and stone having no power to save.

Without the words and the works of Jesus, men and women would fear life more than they fear death.

I know a fine man who remembers as a boy being given one line in the Christmas cantata at his church. On cue he was to appear suddenly before the congregation and declare those majestic words of Jesus: "It is I, be not afraid!" (Matt. 14: 27). But stage fright drove the line from his memory as he stammered: "It's me, and I'm scared to death!"

If Christ had not come, we would all be scared to death—of life. But Christ has come. It's a wonderful life.

As If . . .

And yet, millions of persons live as if Christ has not come. "If I had not come and spoken to them," said Jesus, "they would have no sin, but now they have no excuse for their sin" (John 15:22).

And what is sin? Sin is unbelief in God, and the symptom of sin is human ignorance. Sin distorts the powers of reason.

Speaking of his former life as a terrorist who tried to destroy the church, the apostle Paul confessed: "I was formerly a blasphemer and persecutor, an insolent man. And yet I was shown mercy because I acted ignorantly in unbelief" (1 Tim. 1:13). Human badness is attributed to human blindness.

The prophet Isaiah once compared men and women—created in the image of God with the capacity to think God's thoughts after him—with the lowly ox and ass driven by instinct. The comparison is not complimentary: "The ox knows its owner, and the ass its master's crib. But Israel does not know; my people do not consider" (Isa. 1:3).

"Dumb as an ox" . . . "Stubborn as a mule!" . . . Yet, these creatures of the animal kingdom appear to know more by instinct than men and women know by reason and revelation.

Therefore, the sin of ignorance is a form of belatedness. It is clinging to the darkness after the light has come. It is turning back the calendar to the world of B.C.—before Christ—after the angels have announced *"Anno Domini"*—the year of our Lord.

One Christmas season at Lenox Square in Atlanta, that great cathedral of consumerism, a merchant bore his witness behind his window. A huge manger scene built to scale replaced luxury goods. The star in the east cast its beam against the Light of the World lying in a manger. The holy family and wise men from afar knelt in adoration. And within the shadows of the stable, shepherds and their flocks bowed low.

A father and his young son walked hurriedly past that window. The boy suddenly stopped, transfixed, his nose against the plate glass window. The father soon returned and said to the boy angrily, "Didn't I tell you to keep up with me?"

But the boy responded, "Look Dad, it's the Baby Jesus! It's the Baby Jesus!"

Grabbing the boy by the shoulder and jerking him forward, he said hatefully, "Come on. We don't have time for that sort of thing!"

The ox knows its owner and the ass his master's crib by instinct. But after twenty centuries of the propagation of the words and works of Jesus, men and women don't have time for Christ? They may not have time, but they have no excuse. Their anger fulfills the ancient law of Scripture, "They hated me without a cause" (John 15:25b).

I return to the evangelist's original question: What if Christ had not come? Our planet would go on spinning, eclipsed by increasing darkness and ignorance.

But Christ has come. Both his words and his works prevail. "And the light shines in the darkness, and the darkness did not [overpower] it" (John 1:5).

Recently, Dr. Fred Craddock, retired professor of preaching at Emory University, spoke to pastors and chaplains at our medical center.[3] He reminded us that Christ is already present in the cancer ward, the emergency room, the trauma room. Our job is simply to remain faithful.

He recalled a beloved family whose rather "sheltered" daughter went off to the University of Texas and majored in journalism. After graduation she interviewed for a job with a newspaper in Huntsville.

"Now, you'll have to cover the society page, attend weddings, photograph all the beautiful people."

"Oh, I can do that. I'd love to do that. I'm trained to do that."

"But that's not all. You will also have to cover death row. You know the state's execution chamber is located here, and Texas executes more prisoners than any other state. You'll have to cover those stories."

"I didn't major in criminal justice," said the young reporter, "but I'll do my best."

And she did. She visited death row. She became acquainted with the warden and the prisoners. She got to know a young prisoner, Johnnie Nobles, and followed his appeals process all the way to the Supreme Court. Late one afternoon she had a message from the warden: "Johnnie's appeal was turned down by the high court; execution is set for 6 a.m. He requests that you visit."

She went to death row. The atmosphere was tense as the death chamber was prepared. The tray that had contained the prisoner's last meal sat empty on the table. Finally, it was time to leave. She said in a choking voice: "Johnnie, I'll be on my knees praying for you in the morning, Is there anything I could do before I go?"

"Yes," there is one thing," said Johnnie. "Would you sing my favorite song?"

"Well, I'm not a music major, but if I know it, I'll try. What is your favorite song?"

"Silent Night," said he. "I've loved that song since I was a child. If only I could hear it one more time."

Suddenly, it was Christmas Eve on death row. Condemned men heard again the familiar words of the Savior's birth as written by Joseph Mohr:

Silent night, holy night,
All is calm, all is bright.
Round yon virgin mother and child!
Holy Infant so tender and mild,
Sleep in heavenly peace,
Sleep in heavenly peace.

Silent night, holy night,
Wondrous star, lend thy light;
With the angels let us sing
Alleluia to our King;
Christ the Savior is born,
Christ the Savior is born.

God's mysterious presence can penetrate even those haunts of human wretchedness and narrow cells of judicial condemnation. Therefore, our calling is to remain faithful.

What If . . .

What if Mary had not gone to Bethlehem and delivered her baby? But she did. What if Jesus had not gone to Calvary and died for our sins according to the Scriptures? But he did. What if that young reporter had not gone to death row? But she did. What if you had not been born? But you were. That fact and the grace of God make you a candidate for "a wonderful life."

A Prayer

> O God, the world in which we are called to live is not
> one of black and white but of different grays; not of
> truth and falsehood but the compounding of both; not
> of good and evil but the ambiguities that divide them;
> not of light and darkness but the twilight between. Give
> us, therefore, wisdom this day in our choices, courage
> in our decisions, and a continual discontent with any-
> thing less than the best that Thou has revealed to us so
> wondrously in Jesus Christ. Amen
>
>   —John McIntyre[4]

Notes

[1] *Leading Lives That Matter*, ed. Mark R. Schwehn and Dorothy C. Bass (Grand Rapids: Wm. B. Eerdmans Publishing, 2006), 117.

[2] Ibid., 118.

[3] Northeast Georgia Medical Center, Gainesville, Georgia.

[4] John McIntyre, *Theology After the Storm* (Grand Rapids: Wm. B. Eerdmans Publishing, 1997), 258. Used by permission.

CHAPTER 9

BEYOND BLIND AMBITION ...
The Temptation of Jesus Christ and the Damnation of Theron Ware

Luke 4:5-8

Then the devil . . . showed [Jesus] all the kingdoms of the world in a moment of time.

—*Luke 4:5*

"On a clear day," declares a popular song, "you can see forever." In a moment of time, declares the devil to Jesus, you can see for now the glittering wonders of the world and the gigantic kingdoms that created them. Everything—as far to the east with its Hanging Gardens of Babylon, and as far to the west with its Temple of Artemis at Ephesus—everything shall be yours—for a price.

The temptation of Jesus Christ exposes the seduction of places and positions and possessions that can penetrate the holiest of callings with the corruption of careerism.

The Damnation of Theron Ware

Perhaps the finest commentary on this biblical text is Harold Frederic's novel, *The Damnation of Theron Ware*. In fact, Methodist bishop Will Willimon says he would require all candidates for ministry to read the novel prior to graduation from seminary or divinity school. Frederic, a journalist with *The New York Times*, traces the meteoric rise of a gifted preacher who eventually plunges into moral and vocational ruin. The novel is both a prophecy of the twentieth century and a self-fulfilling prophecy of the author.[1]

The story begins as Theron Ware and his wife, Alice, arrive in the mythical midwestern town of Octavius to begin their third appointment in the Methodist system. Ware's preaching prowess has recently mesmerized members of the annual Methodist conference, but because of denominational politics he misses an appointment to a fashionable city church. Octavius, with many Irish Catholics but few Methodists, is at best for him a steppingstone to something better.

Soon, the preacher is suffocating in the petty atmosphere of parish gossip about his wife's clothes, the constant niggling over the expenses of the pastorium, and the carping of trustees who demand "no dictionary words" be used in their pulpit. Ware's subsequent restlessness and resentment render him vulnerable to three seductive personalities in town who, over a period of time, show him the kingdoms of the world.

Doctor Ledsmar

Doctor Ledsmar is the town's physician who has given up the practice of medicine for medical research. This former general practitioner represents the kingdom of science—but without reverence. Ledsmar resembles the judge in one of Jesus' parables who did not fear God and did not respect people (Luke 18:2). Thus, the doctor is the town's resident agnostic. His character is as reptilian as the creatures caged in his laboratory.

Theron Ware's education has not prepared him to parry the verbal assaults of this soulless scientist. Ledsmar belongs to that sobering figure of speech employed by the psalmist: "serpents that will not be charmed" (Ps. 58:5). But it is the preacher who is charmed by the serpent!

Furthermore, the doctor harbors a horrible secret: he is performing medical experiments on his Chinese servant that are slowly killing the man—all in the interest of healing and advancing medical science.

Within three decades, in Germany, following the publication of this novel, the fictional Doctor Ledsmar will be "reincarnated" in the notorious physician, Josef Mengele, remembered as "the angel of death."[2] Mengele and his medical colleagues will kill thousands of patients in the interest of a perverted science. Doctor Ledsmar fulfills the prophecy of the Russian novelist, Dostoevsky, who said in his *Grand Inquisitor.* "If there is no God, everything is permitted."

But Theron Ware harbors a perilous naiveté: he does not sense the presence of evil in others or the potential for evil in himself.

Father Forbes

Father Forbes, pastor of the Catholic parish, symbolizes the kingdom of religion—but without revelation. This affable priest is a religious professional, but he is not a religious man. Theron Ware is fascinated by this consummate clerical sophisticate. The learned priest, speaking with authority, gives Ware a post-graduate course in the German school of higher biblical criticism. Father Forbes suggests to the preacher that Abraham probably never existed as an historic person; therefore, Forbes has given up preaching. He still celebrates the mystery of religion but not its message. For this priest, there is no message. Thus from priestly lips Theron Ware hears again the seductive voice of the tempter who whispers, "Has God indeed said . . . ?" (Gen. 3:36).

Beneath this baleful influence, Theron Ware neglects "the spiritual gift . . . which was bestowed . . . through prophetic utterance with the laying on of hands by the presbytery" (1 Tim. 3:14). He loses all interest in Methodist doctrine. When Alice Ware, doubting her own salvation, turns to her husband for the bread of assurance, she is given a stone of skepticism. On Sundays at the Methodist church, the hungry sheep look up but are not fed.[3]

Harold Frederic insightfully comments on the erosion of faith in this fictional creation:

> Father Forbes could talk coolly about the Christ-myth
> without ceasing to be a priest, and apparently a very
> active and devoted priest. Evidently there was an intel-
> lectual world, a world of culture and grace, of lofty
> thoughts and the inspiring communion of real knowl-
> edge, where creeds were not of importance; and where
> men asked of each other, not "Is your soul saved?" but
> "Is your mind well furnished?"[4]

Theron Ware had become a citizen of that world without any serious reflection on what he was giving up: the integrity of his soul and his high and holy calling.

Celia Madden

Celia Madden completes the triumvirate of the temptation of Theron Ware. Beautiful socialite and heiress to the town fortune, Celia incarnates the kingdom of beauty—but without the beauty of holiness. Her communion is the cult of the Greeks with a theology of the strong and beautiful.

The Madden mansion is filled with the music of Chopin and the artworks of Raphael. Celia's lissome figure, adorned with an imported wardrobe, is as graceful as the sculptured figurines on her grand piano. Compared with this glamorous aesthete, poor Alice Ware appears uninteresting to her husband. Besotted with infatuation, deluded by his own vanity, Ware believes Celia, this beautiful worldling, is romantically interested in him.

When he finally confesses his love for Celia, Ware is rudely rebuffed by her rejection and searing assessment of his character. Says she, "What you took for improvement was really degeneration!"[5]

Thus rejected, Ware plunges into a mental breakdown, becomes suicidal, and resigns from the church. A forgiving wife and a simple couple in the congregation, "Brother and Sister Soulsby," stand by their man until he finds a sales job in Seattle. The ministry records another casualty, caused not by sexual intrigue or honest doubt, but by upward mobility: "What you took for improvement was really degeneration!"

The Temptation of Jesus Christ

In the temptation of Jesus Christ, God's "prime minister" moves from upward mobility—all the kingdoms of the world—to downward humility. As the eyes of Jesus focus on the glittering wonders of the world, his inward disposition is "fixed downward" toward the invisible Kingdom of God. During the days of his flesh his pathway will reverse the trajectory of Lincoln "from the White House to the log cabin."[6] The apostle Paul documents his downward descent in these words:

> Have this mind in yourselves which was also in Christ
> Jesus, who, although he existed in the form of God, did
> not regard equality with God a thing to be grasped, but
> emptied himself, taking the form of a bond-servant, and
> being made in the likeness of men. And being found in

appearance as a man, he humbled himself by becoming obedient to the point of death, even death on a cross. Therefore also God highly exalted him . . . (Phil. 2:5-9a NASB)

The late Richard John Newhaus, a former Lutheran pastor, Roman Catholic priest, author, and publisher, suggested that Jesus practiced a model of ministry worthy of emulation: he chose those ministries that others did not choose.[7] Such a choice delivers the high calling from succumbing to the seduction of blind ambition. On the road, Jesus touches a leper whom others shun (Mark 1:41). He blesses a child whom others ignore (Mark 10:16). In the upper room he washes soiled feet that others refuse to touch (John 13:5). In the end he takes up a cross from which others flee (Matt. 26:56).

By choosing ministries that others do not choose, Jesus reconfigures the pattern of ministry to include the unwanted, the unwashed, and the unblessed. Such downward humility avoids the carnality of competition and the jaundice of jealousy that so disfigure ministry.

This model of ministry would open doors to those who have been shut out, and would open the doors of the church to new seasons of refreshing.

When Francis of Assisi appeared before Pope Innocent, he sought permission for the order of the Franciscans to preach the gospel to the poor. Francis was introduced to Innocent by the pope's nephew, Cardinal Ugolino, and the resplendent pope was put off by Francis' eccentric and uncouth appearance. He told Francis to go and play with the pigs, where he belonged. To the pope's consternation, Francis took him literally and reappeared the next day in the consistory caked in pig dung. The pope hastily granted his requests! Francis had taken humility to a new level. But the poor heard the gospel, and Christ's church was repaired.[8]

And yet, are there not coveted and strategic places in the kingdom —symbolized by a cardinal's cap, a bishop's miter, a theology deanship, a tall steeple pastorate? Yes. There are such positions, and they require their incumbents' extraordinary gifts. But, insisted Newhaus, such positions are achieved not by ambition, but by obedience.[9]

Pope Benedict XVI was elected vicar of Christ at the age of 81. He later disclosed that he did not seek the office, but the office sought him. Like the apostle Paul, the vicar of Christ was not disobedient to the heavenly vision (Acts 26:19). But equally inspiring are the deeds of the very gifted, who, through obedience, choose those places that others would not choose.

Doctor Paul Brand, British subject, son of missionary parents, orthopedic surgeon, world authority on Hanson's disease, directs the only leprosarium in the continental United States. Located near Carville, Louisiana, on the banks of the Mississippi River, amid crumbling crawfish cafés and petrochemical factories, is a hospital for lepers. There, Director Paul Brand teaches his patients that pain is really a gift from God. But on Wednesdays the doctor becomes a preacher. Brand conducts a midweek prayer service, and Mrs. Brand directs the choir. A recent visitor, author Philip Yancy, reported five persons in the choir and eight in the audience. But Yancey's memory was seared forever by the experience: "To that motley crew, Brand proceeded to deliver an address worthy of Westminster Abby. Obviously, he had spent hours meditating and praying over that one sermon. It mattered not that we were a tiny cluster of half-dead nobodies in a sleepy bayou chapel."[10]

What if Frederic Forsyth, like Philip Yancey, had encountered Paul Brand? Doctor Brand, unlike Doctor Ledsmar, practices the kingdom of science with a reverence for God and respect for people. Unlike Father Forbes, Brand has not given up on preaching, even to a tiny cluster of half-dead nobodies. Like Celia Madden, Doctor Brand is also an aesthete, but he finds the beauty of holiness amid a community disfigured by disease and polluted by chemicals. Brand's "success" is portrayed in the apostle Paul's "failure": [As] sorrowful, yet always rejoicing; as poor, yet making many rich; as having nothing, yet possessing all things (2 Cor. 6:10).

The popular song got it right: "On a clear day you can see forever." On the day of temptation, Jesus saw beyond a moment in time to an event in eternity. He saw, and heard the angel declare: "The kingdom of the world has become the kingdom of our Lord and his Christ; and he will reign forever and ever" (Rev. 11:15b). Therefore, Jesus refused to worship the devil to acquire the kingdoms of the world because they were already his!

When you and I seek first the Lord and his kingdom, all other kingdoms will eventually find us. The person who has God for his treasure has all things in one.[11] In the end, kingdom people own nothing but possess everything.

A Prayer

> O Lord, who has taught us that to gain the whole world
> and to lose our soul is great folly, grant us the grace so to
> lose ourselves that we may truly find ourselves anew in
> the lure of grace, and so to forget ourselves that we may
> be remembered in your kingdom. Amen.
>
> —Reinhold Niebuhr[12]

Notes

[1]Harold Frederic, *The Damnation of Theron Ware, or Illumination* (New York: Stone and Kimball, 1896). According to a note in the fly leaf of this volume, while Frederic was on assignment to the London bureau of *The New York Times*, he left his family and took up with a woman who practiced Christian Science. When Frederic became ill, she refused to call a physician and consequently he died from neglect.

[2]Martin Gilbert, *The Second World War: A Complete History* (London: Folio Society, 1989), 503-504.

[3]John Milton used this image for the preacher's neglect.

[4]Horton Davies, *A Mirror of the Mystery in Modern Novels* (New York: Oxford University Press, 1959), 71-78.

[5]Ibid., 77.

[6]Paul Scherer is responsible for the phrase, "From White House to log cabin."

[7]Richard John Neuhaus, *Freedom for Ministry* (Grand Rapids: Wm. B. Erdmanns Publishing, 1992), 239.

[8]Ermon Dufey, *Saints and Sinners* (London: The Folio Society, 2009), 162.

[9]Neuhaus, 240.

[10]Philip Yancey, *Soul Survivor: How Thirteen Unlikely Mentors Helped My Faith Survive the Church* (New York: Doubleday, 2003), 61.

[11]A. W. Tozer, *The Pursuit of God* (Camp Hill, PA: Christian Publications, Inc., 2009), 19.

[12]Reinhold Niebuhr, *Justice and Mercy*, ed. Ursula Niebuhr (New York: Harper & Row, 1974) 11.

CHAPTER 10

BEYOND AFFLUENCE ...
Empty Chairs at Empty Tables

Luke 16:19-31

There's a grief that can't be spoken.
There's a pain that goes on and on.
Empty chairs at empty tables,
Now my friends are dead and gone.

Phantom faces at the window,
Phantom shadows on the floor,
Empty chairs at empty tables,
Where my friends will be no more.
                    —*Les Miserables*[1]

In Luke 16, Jesus tells a parable about a rich man and a beggar, a parable made poignant by empty chairs at empty tables—and missing guests. The story unfolds in two scenes.

Scene One: Somewhere in Time

A rich man lives in a gated community with all the amenities, "safe and secure from all alarm." The man is nameless. Tradition, however, dubs him "*Dives*," the Latin word for "wealth." The name is appropriate. This man's life is defined by his wealth. His obituary will eventually bear but three words: "He was rich." Not "he was kind" or "he was wise," but "he was rich." Indeed, Dives believes that life is constituted by the abundance of one's possessions.

Inside the gated community the centerpiece of the rich man's existence is the dining room table. There, Dives presides as the genial host, "elegant and swellegant,"[2] dressed in purple and fine linen. In taste, he is a gourmet of fine cuisine; in affiliation, he probably belongs to the Sadducee Party.

The Sadducees represent the "old money" crowd, who made their wealth the old-fashioned way: they inherited it! The Sadducees control the temple, and believe neither in all the scriptures nor in the resurrection of the dead. They do believe in the good life, in the here and now.

Dives would echo Jack Welch, former CEO of General Electric. A reporter asked Welch, following his open-heart surgery, if he had an epiphany. Welch replied: "Yes, I had an epiphany. I vowed that I would never drink another bottle of wine costing less than $100."[3]

Meanwhile, outside the gated community, protected from burglars and panhandlers, is a beggar. His name is Lazarus, which means "God is my help." Lazarus belongs to the righteous poor, who look beyond the hills for help from God. Unfortunately, he is receiving little help from the people of God. Daily, Lazarus scrounges for scraps that fall from the rich man's table. Bread sustains the poor and provides the rich with napkins on which to wipe greasy hands. The crumbs are cast outside the gated community and subsequently consumed by scavenging dogs that slobber on the sores of the beggar.

Life is not fair. Some have so much, but others so little.

"There's a grief that can't be spoken; there's a pain that goes on and on."

A phantom face appears at the window of the gated community; a phantom shadow falls across the floor of the elegant dining room table. The face and the shadow belong to the beggar; the grief and the pain belong to God. There sits an empty chair at the table. Lazarus is missing!

In the land flowing with milk and honey, Moses laid down the law of God: "For the poor shall never cease from the land. Therefore, I command you saying, 'You shall open your hand wide to your brother, to your poor and your needy in your land'" (Deut. 15:11).

In the heart of God and in the economy of God there is a place for every person at Earth's table. But Lazarus was never included at the table. "There's a grief that can't be spoken . . . empty chairs at empty tables."

Life is not fair, but death is democratic. Both Dives and Lazarus appear in the obituary. The beggar dies and, like the impoverished

Mozart, is probably dumped in a pauper's grave worthy of one shovelful of lime. The rich man also dies, but he is buried in a proper manner. Men die, usually, as they have lived. The one who fared sumptuously every day is given a funeral fit for a pharaoh. Now, inside the gated community sits Dives' empty chair at the table.

Scene Two: Somewhere Beyond

A great reversal has occurred. The first has become last, and the last, first. Lazarus is comforted; Dives is tormented. In scene one, Lazarus is a beggar. In scene two, Dives is the beggar.

The centerpiece of scene two, as in scene one, is a dining room table occupied by a rich man and a beggar. Abraham is the second rich man in the story, even richer than Dives. But Abraham's life is defined not by his wealth, but by his faith. Abraham believed God and was declared a righteous man.

At the messianic banquet in the beyond, the righteous poor and the righteous rich are among the blessed. Lazarus—borne by angelic pallbearers into the abode of the blessed—leans on the bosom of Abraham, just as the Beloved Disciple at the Last Supper leaned on the bosom of Jesus. Such spiritual intimacy is synonymous with heaven's ecstasy.

But in scene two, again an empty chair sits at the messianic table. Dives is missing. He now stares across a chasm wider than the Grand Canyon that is fixed, final and forever. "There's a grief that can't be spoken."

What are we to make of this?

Biblical scholar Reinhold Niebuhr reminds us that parables are symbolic and "if we are wise, we shall not gage the furniture of heaven nor the temperature of hell." Properly so, since neither of the New Testament words for "heaven" nor "hell" appears in the parable.[4] Rather than casting Dives in heaven or hell, we might say that he made choices whose consequences led eventually to an inexorable finality.

What, then, is Dives' failure? His wealth? No. Dives exposes the anatomy of greed. His hand is closed to the poor because his heart is closed to God. Like his brothers on earth, Dives had Moses and the prophets, but he did not hear them. Dives was not only rich in wealth, but he also belonged to a community rich in revelation.

The apostle Paul asks what advantage belongs to the Jewish heritage. Why, every advantage, of course: the oracles of God, the sacred Scripture, Moses, and the prophets (Rom. 3:2). But Dives remained deaf.

The Good Shepherd, the great evangel Jesus Christ, devotes his mission to "the lost sheep of the house of Israel." He warns the privileged of being presumptuous about their rich tradition:

> There will be weeping and gnashing of teeth when you
> see Abraham and Isaac and Jacob and all the prophets
> in the Kingdom of God, but you, yourselves, cast out.
> And they will come from east and west, and from north
> and south, and will recline at the table in the Kingdom
> of God. And behold, some are last who will be first, and
> some are first who will be last. (Luke 13:28-30)

At the messianic banquet in the Kingdom of God, Dives' chair is empty and God is grieved. The parable ends by probing the possibility of persuasion. Dives makes a final request of Abraham: Would he commission Lazarus, the beggar, and send him back from the dead? Dressed in grave clothes, the beggar might frighten Dives' five brothers from their affliction of "affluenza."

Abraham declines. "They have Moses and the prophets . . . if they do not listen to Moses and the prophets, neither will they be persuaded if someone rises from the dead." We, too, have Moses and the prophets—but much more. We have Moses and the prophets, and the Gospels and the Epistles—but still much more.

Someone Has Risen from the Dead!

The story is there in the Holy Scriptures. The word of God is sufficient for a saving faith. A saving faith comes from hearing and obeying the Word of God. The witness of those who have encountered the Living Word and have been changed by the encounter is compelling.

One of the most effective preachers of our times was the late Carl Bates of Charlotte, North Carolina. As a young man, Carl forsook his religious roots in the Mississippi topsoil to run through the underworld of New Orleans. There, the wages of sin suddenly came due and Carl could not pay. In despair, he checked into a downtown hotel, rode the elevator to the eleventh floor, turned the key to the room, and opened the window to the concrete parapet to make his final exit.

But glancing back, he saw on the nightstand a Gideon Bible. An inner voice said, "Take up and read; take up and read." Carl Bates took up the book and in its pages met a man. A mysterious presence haunted that upper room in New Orleans, who once haunted that upper room in Jerusalem:

> Now (the Stranger) said to them (men in despair): "These are my words, which I spoke to you while I was still with you, that all the things which are written about me in the Law of Moses and the Prophets and the Psalms must be fulfilled." Then he opened their minds to understand the Scriptures. (Luke 24:44-45 NASB)

Carl Bates checked out of that hotel in New Orleans and soon checked into Southern Seminary in Louisville, Kentucky, where devoted teachers opened his mind to understand the Scriptures.

Consequently, we, too, have Moses and the prophets. We have the written word and the Living Word. Their message is an invitation: "O taste and see that the Lord is good" (Ps. 34:8).

It's too late for Dives and his brothers, but it's not too late for you and me. Jesus has gone before us to prepare a place at the table. Lazarus will be there. Abraham will be there. Jesus wants you and me to be there.

In the economy of God, there is a place for every person at earth's table. By the grace of God there is a place for every person at heaven's banquet. Please, make sure your chair is not left empty.

A Prayer

> Remember not, Lord Christ, our offenses nor the offenses of our forefathers; neither reward us according to our sins. From all oppression, conspiracy, and rebellion; from violence, battle, and murder; and from dying suddenly and unprepared, Good Lord, deliver us. Amen.[5]
>
> —*The Book of Common Prayer*

Notes

[1]Alan Boubill Music LTD (ASCAP). Permission to quote requested from Music Theatre International. See also http://www.metralyrics.com/emptychairsatempty-tables-lyrics-lesmiserables.html.

[2]Karl Menninger, *Whatever Became of Sin?* (New York: Hawthorne Books, 1973), 202.

[3]Chuck Colson, *The Good Life* (Carol Stream, IL: Tyndale House Publishers, 2005), 52.

[4]Craig Blomberg, *Interpreting the Parables* (Leicester: Apollos, 1990), 203-208.

[5]Adapted from "The Great Litany."

CHAPTER 11

BEYOND VIOLENCE ...
Forgiven!

Matthew 18:21-35 (NASB)

*Lord, how often shall my brother sin against me and I forgive him?
Up to seven times?*

—Matthew 18:21 (NASB)

The gravestone in the cemetery behind the white frame church contained only one word. No name. No elegy. Just "Forgiven." Passers-by pondered the sin that had evoked that simple epitaph. Was the deceased perhaps a prodigal child who returned home, clothes and countenance soiled with the filth of some far country? Had his confession been kissed away by a parent's pardon? Had the departed once worn a scarlet letter that symbolized a fleshly sin of passion that had scandalized the community? Whatever the offense, and whomever the offender, the entire biography of one person, known only to God, was borne by one word: Forgiven.[1]

During the days of the Lord's flesh, the apostle Peter apparently encountered a sinning brother, not in the cemetery, but in the assembly: "Lord, how often shall my brother sin against me and I forgive him? Up to seven times?" (Matt.18:21 NASB). The Jewish rabbis, like the umpires in baseball, declare, "Three strikes and you're out!" Following that indictment, the offender is to be treated as a Gentile and tax collector (Matt. 18:17).

Would Jesus raise the ante from three strikes to seven? The Lord sweeps aside the suggestion. Forgiveness requires not a scorekeeper or a rulebook, but a magnanimous soul. Whereupon, Jesus tells a parable, "a small masterpiece of dramatic choreography in three tightly integrated scenes."[2] The three scenes reveal three characters: a king and two slaves, whose behavior is held in stark contrast.

Scene One: Forgiven

The parable compares the kingdom of heaven with a king who wishes to settle accounts with his debtor-slaves. An audit of the books reveals that one slave has embezzled the sum of ten thousand talents.

Ten thousand talents is estimated at approximately ten million dollars in silver content, but worth much more in buying power. King Herod the Great received annually from all Jewish provinces only nine hundred talents in tax revenues. Ten thousand talents represent "the largest amount imaginable."[3] The appropriate word for such a sum is enormous!

A Jewish audience upon hearing the parable of the talents would immediately think of Egyptian pharaohs who buried their enormous wealth with the dead.[4] This fact was impressed upon American audiences who witnessed King Tut's tomb on tour and the lavish display of enormous wealth.

And who could ever restore so enormous a debt? To sell the slave who owed that sum, along with his wife and children and their possessions, would hardly restore a fraction of the ten thousand talents.

Such an enormous debt can only be resolved by extravagant forgiveness. Therefore, "The Lord of that slave felt compassion and released him and forgave him the debt" (Matt. 18:27 NASB).

The apostle Paul put that enormous financial transaction into a doctrinal declaration: "And the law came in that the transgression might increase; but where sin increased, grace abounded all the more" (Rom. 5:20 NASB). Forgiven!

Scene Two: Unforgiven

In the second scene, the slave who was forgiven the sum of ten thousand talents encounters a fellow slave who owes him the paltry pittance of one hundred denarii—less than a hundred dollars. Grabbing his debtor in a chokehold, the forgiven one shouts: "Pay back what you owe!" The poor man slips loose and falls to the ground gasping for breath, pleading, "Have patience with me and I will repay you." But mercy received is mercy denied. The hapless slave is cast into debtor's prison for less than a few dollars where he, and presumably his family, will face utter ruin and remain unforgiven.

Thus the parable pivots on the contrasting behavior of a king who forgives his slave ten thousand talents and the slave who refuses to forgive a fellow debtor a paltry pound of flesh. If the final work of grace is a graceful person, what has happened to this graceless man?

Perhaps the more pertinent question is rather, what has not happened to him? Apparently the proper answer is: the man forgiven ten thousand talents received forgiveness but did not experience forgiveness. The display of so enormous an act of grace left him unmoved, unrepentant, and unchanged.

From the cross, Jesus offered a prayer of general amnesty: "Father, forgive them, for they know not what they do" (Luke 23:34 NASB). Included in that prayer were two thieves with whom he was numbered. But one thief rebelled and the other repented (Luke 23:42). Both transgressors received forgiveness, but only one experienced forgiveness.

The experience of forgiving grace is almost always a searing and sometimes a shattering experience. Harry Emerson Fosdick, the grand old liberal preacher who confessed to delivering fundamentalist sermons, lived up to that claim in his sermon, "Forgiveness of Sins."[5] In it he took up Jesus' question to the paralytic man in the city of Capernaum, "Which is easier; to say, . . . your sins are forgiven or to say, arise and take up your pallet and walk?" (Mark 2:9 NASB). The answer is clear: even for Jesus, the physical miracle of healing is much easier to perform than the moral miracle of forgiveness. To say, "Rise and walk," is easier than to say, "Your sins are forgiven." Why? Jesus found it hard to forgive because forgiveness is such a terrific experience for the person who is forgiven.[6]

Anyone who takes so searing a possibility of pardon lightheartedly is certainly one who has never been forgiven; and anyone who takes the potential pardon of another hardheartedly, like the slave in the parable, has never experienced forgiveness. Unforgiven!

Scene Three: Forgiven/Unforgiven

In scene three, other slaves who have witnessed the act of hardhearted violence are deeply grieved and report it to the king, who is also deeply grieved—and angered. Summoning the previous debtor, who makes his third appearance in the parable, the king declares: "You wicked slave. I forgave you all the debt because you entreated me. Should you not have had mercy on your fellow slave as I had mercy on you?" Thereupon, the king cancels the pardon, restores the debt, and turns the debtor over to the torturers who stretch him on the rack. The last scene depicts the final fate and utter ruin of the unforgiving. The parable's punch line? "God will not forgive us our unforgiveness."[7]

In the meantime, the troubled slaves in the parable raise a troubling question for all of us. What becomes of a community in which forgiveness is not practiced? Does that community have a viable future? That question is probed in the award-winning film, *Unforgiven*.

Clint Eastwood portrays William Munny, a man with a violent past. Married to a good woman whose Christian influence compels him to put away his pistols, Munny becomes a pig farmer. But the wife's death from smallpox leaves him bereaved and adrift. One day the pig farmer, like the prodigal son in the hog pen, comes to himself—his violent self. As he straps on his pistols, the audience is signaled the film's central question: Can violence be cured?[8]

Munny's next stop is Big Whiskey, Wyoming, a violent place that practices vengeance. The town has most of the institutions you find anywhere, including a brothel run by women more sinned against than sinning, a saloon that doubles as a courtroom, and a sheriff called "Little Bill." But Little Bill neither serves nor protects; his tin star conceals a sadistic killer.

The film ends in the saloon when Munny, lubricated by liquor and fortified with a shotgun, confronts Little Bill and his henchmen. When the smoke clears, the sheriff lies on the floor wounded and tries to get off, if not the last shot, at least the last word: "I'll see you in hell, William Munny." "Yeah," drawls Munny as he reloads his weapon, "I suppose you will." BAM! The film's dark message? Those who are habituated to violence cannot unlearn it.[9] The last word of the film, like the last word of the parable, is "unforgiven."

And yet, one institution is missing in Big Whiskey. It has no church. If there were a church, the community might have another chance for a future. In church, the community is confronted with the word brother: "If my brother sins against me, how often shall I forgive him?" In church, the community is taught to pray: "Forgive us our debts as we forgive our debtors." In church, the community learns the meaning of mercy and the blessing bestowed on those who give and receive mercy. If Big Whiskey had had a church, the film's last word might have been "forgiven."

Therefore, in the end, Matthew's Jesus measures forgiveness, both divine and human, by the old math. The king's cancellation of the debt of ten million talents makes God's forgiveness of sinners unimaginable; Jesus' computation of forgiveness toward brothers at seventy-times-seven makes any act of unforgiveness unthinkable.

Consequently, parables provoke the mind to ponder the unthinkable. They function as "a rake in the grass"[10]; they appear harmless—until you step on one! Suddenly, the handle flies up and figuratively hits you in the face, leaving you startled but maybe smarter. Thus the parable of the unforgiving slave leaves the hearer with an appalling alternative to forgiveness: Not even God will forgive our unforgiveness.

And yet, such a stark conclusion raises a more troubling question: If God's forgiveness of me hinges on my forgiveness of others, is that not finally a salvation of works and not grace? What then becomes of "For by grace you have been saved through faith and that not of yourselves, it is the gift of God" (Eph. 2:8 NASB)? Such questions require closure.

In a recent broadcast of his morning sermon over the Trinity Network, San Diego pastor David Jeremiah distinguished between judicial and relational forgiveness—the former is fixed; the latter is fluid—by telling the following story.

When he was seventeen and his father was away on business, David took the keys to the family's Chrysler Newport and went joy-riding in the country. Alas, upon meeting a farmer on a tractor, he drove into a ditch where the rocky embankment cut a huge gash in the side of the car.

When David's father returned and saw the damaged car, he entered the house and asked: "David, did you do this?" David replied: "Yes, sir, I did." His father said nothing.

After two days of deadly silence David went to his father's office, confessed the whole story, and asked forgiveness. Whereupon his father forgave him, embraced him, and then sat him down to talk about earning money to repair the damaged car.

The father's forgiveness was not judicial, but relational. Judicially, David was his father's son and nothing would ever change that fact. But relationally, he was estranged from his father and the impasse could be resolved only by confession, forgiveness, and reparation where possible.

The parable in Matthew about the unforgiving slave is about relational forgiveness. We are saved through grace alone, and nothing will change that fact. Therefore, such probing and ponderings confirm one truth: Relationships are sacred—and fragile! They endure only through continual acts of forgiving grace. For indeed, the final work of God's grace is a graceful person.

A Prayer

How can your pardon reach and bless
The unforgiving heart
That broods on wrongs
And will not let old bitterness depart?

In blazing light your cross reveals
The truth we dimly knew:
What trivial debts are owed to us;
How great our debt to you.
Amen.

—Rosamond E. Herklots[11]

Notes

[1]Ralph Murry, veteran Baptist pastor in Knoxville, Tennessee, was the source of this reference.

[2]John Dominic Crossan, *In Parables: The Challenge of the Historical Jesus* (New York: Harper & Row, 1973), 106.

[3]David Hill, *The Gospel of Matthew* (Greenwood, SC: Attic Press, 1978), 278.

[4]Craig L. Blomberg, *Interpreting the Parables* (Leicester: Apollos Press, 1990), 242.

[5]Harry Emerson Fosdick, *Riverside Sermons* (New York: Harper Brothers, 1958), 292.

[6]Ibid., 298.

[7]Crossan, 105.

[8]L. Gregory Jones, *Embodying Forgiveness: A Theological Analysis* (Grand Rapids: Wm. B. Erdmanns Publishing, 1995), 73.

[9]Ibid., 76.

[10]Source unknown.

[11]www.hymnary.org/person/herklots-RI. Rosamond E. Herklots (b. Masuri, India, 1905; d. Bromley Kent, England, 1987) wrote this prayer-hymn after digging weeds from her garden and thinking how bitterness, hatred, and resentment are like poisonous weeds growing in the Christian garden of life. This prayer is acutely conscious of Jesus' calculation of forgiveness at seventy-times-seven times.

CHAPTER 12

BEYOND INDIFFERENCE ...
The Empty Windows

Luke 10:25-37

And who is my neighbor?
—Luke 10:29

I sit and look out upon all the sorrows of the world, . . . All the
meanness and agony without end, . . . I . . . see, hear, and am silent.
—Walt Whitman[1]

The ordination council and the nervous candidate for ministry met in
an upper room overlooking the city. Members of the council asked the
ordinand the usual questions to determine fitness for ministry:

- "Please tell us of your experience of the call to preach the gospel."
- "What do you believe about the inspiration of scripture?"
- "What academic preparation do you plan to complete to fulfill your
  calling?"

Both the questions and answers were predictable. But one veteran minister is remembered for always asking but one question. After compelling
the candidate to go to the window and look out, he would then ask,
"What do you see? Describe for us what you see outside the window."
The candidate would answer, "Well . . . I . . . uh . . . I see a woman walking to the post office with a packet of letters—probably a secretary." "Is
that all you see—a secretary?" "Well . . . uh . . . I see a man with a brief-
case, heading to the courthouse—probably a lawyer." "But does lawyer
really define that man? Surely you see more than a mere lawyer." By this

time, the fledging minister is beginning to catch on: "Now I get it. I see a woman created in the image of God. I see a man for whom Christ died. I see a city for which Christ wept." "Good," says the veteran minister, "that's good. Always remember: ministry begins at the window."[2]

Indeed it does. Where we stand determines what we see; what we see determines what we do. Some believe that on judgment day our eyes will be examined first.[3] Jesus apparently did: "The lamp of the body is the eye; if therefore your eye is good, your whole body will be full of light" (Matt. 6:22).

Who Is My Neighbor?

A certain lawyer asks Jesus, "Who is my neighbor?" In response, Christ the carpenter constructs with words a window overlooking a rural crime scene. There, a certain man on the road to Jericho is assaulted by a gang of thieves who beat him, strip him of his clothes, and leave him half dead. "Go to the window," says Jesus to the lawyer, "what do you see?"

The certain lawyer sees a certain priest going down the road, who, when he sees the victim, passes by on the other side. Likewise, he sees a Levite, who upon seeing the victim, passes by on the other side. But what do the priest and the Levite see? They see a corpse. After all, the man is half dead. Who can blame them for passing by on the other side? The law of Moses is on their side: "Whoever touches the body of anyone who has died, and does not purify himself, defiles the tabernacle of the Lord, that person shall be cut off from Israel" (Num. 19:13).

Furthermore, according to the levitical law, priests were exempt from burying even their relatives (Lev. 21:1-3). Consequently, these two religious leaders, in avoiding a man half dead, preserve the protocol of their profession and evade the risks of human compassion.

And yet, do not most of us see other persons through the lens of our narrow specialties and hidden agendas? The salesman sees a customer. The lawyer sees a litigant. The surgeon sees a gall bladder. The preacher sees a prospect. The undertaker sees a corpse. Who really sees the whole person?

A Certain Samaritan

Meanwhile, back at the window, the drama continues. A certain Samaritan appears on the scene and, upon seeing the victim, feels compassion. Removing a first-aid kit from his saddlebags, the Samaritan turns the man over, takes his pulse, pours oil and wine into the wounds, and stops the bleeding with a tourniquet. Amazing.

What does this certain Samaritan see in this certain man? He sees an enemy. The enmity of Samaritans and Jews has smoldered for centuries, fueled by rage and race and religion. Samaritans are half-breeds who survived Assyria's invasion of Israel in 722 B.C (2 Kings 17). This quarrel erected a rival Samaritan temple built on Mount Gerazim, which was destroyed in 128 B.C. Josephus, the Jewish historian, blamed its destruction on Samaritan apostasy and treachery.[4]

Surprisingly, upon finding a helpless Jew half dead, the Samaritan doesn't "finish him off." Had "the shoe been on the other foot," the Jew, by law, would have been excused from saving the Samaritan's life.[5] Thus, the only "good Samaritan" is a "dead Samaritan."

What is happening here? Compassion for a fellow human being has risen above race and religion. In a crisis, compassion has appeared from a most unlikely person—an enemy.

Can this happen? Does this happen? Yes. A pastor's daughter lies in a rehab center following a car crash. She has sustained a brain injury along with multiple fractures. The rehab center's rules require that family members must leave by 6 p.m. The nurses are understaffed. The patient is afraid to be left alone. Her parents are anxious.

When the night nurse appears, everyone's fear spikes. The nurse is a Muslim woman from Pakistan. She is wearing traditional headdress and is fasting, for it is the month of Ramadan. The pastor almost panics. Can he leave his Christian daughter in the hands of a Muslim nurse during a war on terror?

The nurse reads their fear and offers assurance: "Now you folks go home and get some rest. Don't worry about your daughter. I'm going to take good care of her. I'll look in on her throughout the night."

And she did take care of her patient, administering not only medications, but also shampoos and manicures. The two women became friends. Human compassion rose above the enmity of religion, politics, and culture.[6]

Now, it is our turn to go to the window. Look out the window. What do you see?

Is Christ Our Neighbor?

Doctor Luke teases our eyes toward the victim who lies half dead in the ditch. Who is that certain man who is lifted onto an ass and borne to an inn? The parable of the good Samaritan brackets the birth and death of Jesus.

At his birth, Jesus is borne on an ass to an inn. "And she brought forth her firstborn son; and she wrapped him in swaddling cloths, and laid him in a manger, because there was no room for them in the inn" (Luke 2:7). At his death, Jesus is stripped and left for dead between two thieves.

Robert Capon finds in this parable the gospel of good news: "The gospel says clearly that we can be saved only by bad examples: by the stupid example of a Samaritan who spends his livelihood on a loser, and by the horrible example of a Savior who, in an excruciating death, lays down his life for his friends."[7]

Who is my neighbor? Go to the window. Look out the window. When you find your neighbor, you may also discover the Savior.

> Then the righteous will answer him, saying, "Lord, when did we see you hungry and feed you, or thirsty and give you drink? When did we see you a stranger and take you in, or naked and clothe you? Or when did we see you sick, or in prison, and come to you?" And the King will answer and say to them, "Assuredly, I say to you, inasmuch as you did it to one of the least of these my brethren, you did it to me." (Matt. 25:37-40)

Therefore, ministry and missions begin at the window. Where we stand determines what we see. What we see determines what we do.

Jimmy Allen, veteran pastor and Christian statesman, believes the church's greatest peril is not in what we are doing, but rather in what we are ignoring. He befriended a Jewish couple in San Antonio, Moshe and Alice Cahanna. Alice, an artist, told her story.

She survived two different death camps in Germany, including Dachau. At the age of eight she was taken from her central European village, along with her parents. They were killed. In her late teens, Alice was on the ship that could find no safe harbor and sailed the Mediterranean Sea, looking for a place to land. The movie *Exodus* told its story. When

Dr. Allen asked Alice to tell her most unforgettable moment, she said, "I remember the empty windows."

"Empty windows?" he asked. "Yes. They came for us that morning. The trucks were parked at the bottom of the hill from our house. I had lived there all my life. As I walked down the hill, I carried the little suitcase with all my possessions they would let me take. They knew! All our neighbors knew. My playmates—they knew. But no one came to the window. As I walked down that hill, I looked and no one came to the windows to see what was happening. I will never forget those empty windows."[8] Later, Alice painted a picture for the pastor titled *Three Empty Windows.*

Therefore, missions begins by putting a face in the empty windows—ours! Everything begins at the window. What do you see? Where is your neighbor? Where is God?

God is in an eight-year-old Jewish child carrying a suitcase to a death camp. God is in a thirty-three-year-old Jewish carpenter carrying a cross to the place of a skull. God is in a Muslim nurse who cares for the daughter of a Christian pastor. It's time to put a face in the window. Indeed, our peril is not in what we are doing, but in what we are ignoring.

For God's sake, for your neighbor's sake, for your soul's sake . . . go to the window.

A Prayer

> We pray thee for those who amid all the knowledge of our day are still without knowledge; for those who hear not the sighs of the children that toil, nor the sobs of such as are wounded because others have made haste to be rich; for those who have never felt the hot tears of the mothers of the poor that struggle vainly against poverty and vice. Arouse them, we beseech thee, from their selfish comfort, and grant them the grace of repentance. Amen.
>
> —Walter Rauschenbusch[9]

Notes

[1]Walt Whitman, *Leaves of Grass* (New York: New American Library, 1964), 227-228.

[2]*What's the Matter with Preaching Today?* ed. Mike Graves (Louisville: Westminster John Knox Press, 2004), 114.

[3]Arnold Uleyn, *Is It I, Lord?: Pastoral Psychology and the Recognition of Guilt* (New York: Holt, Rinehart & Winston, 1969), 144.

[4]Charles Talbert, *Reading Luke: A Literary and Theological Commentary on the Third Gospel* (New York: Crossroad Publishing, 1989), 123.

[5]Ibid.

[6]The rehab center was located in Mount Vernon, Virginia, and the patient was the author's daughter.

[7]Robert Capon, "The Parables of Luke," *Review & Expositor*, 94 (Spring 1997), 272.

[8]Story told at McAfee School of Theology Convocation, Mercer University, Atlanta, Georgia. Used by permission.

[9]Walter Rauschenbusch, *Prayers for Services: A Manual for Leaders of Worship*, ed. Morgan Phelps Noyes (New York: Charles Scribner's Sons, 1934), 150.

CHAPTER 13

BEYOND APOSTASY …
Incomplete Conversions

Luke 11:24-26

And the last state of that man becomes worse than the first.
—Luke 11:26c (NASB)

There is a cartoon in which two tramps are sitting on a park bench. One is an old man with dark circles underneath his eyes and a month's stubble on his chin. He has been around the block—and around the world. The younger tramp, though prematurely bald, is youthful with a baby face. The old tramp begins to muse about religion: "You ever been saved?" he asks. "Yep," says the younger man, "Got saved in Biloxi back in 1963." "But you ain't got no job," observes the old man. "Mebbie you're only half saved."[1]

The old tramp has suddenly become a biblical theologian pondering the profound issue of incomplete conversions. His quip about "half saved" anticipates Jesus' absolute: "He that endures to the end shall be saved" (Matt. 10:22). Therefore, is half saved more hazardous than unsaved? Is a thing half done worse than a thing never begun? That is the question evoked by incomplete conversions.

The Haunted House

Jesus tells a ghost story about a haunted house that got half saved from demon possession. A demon is dramatically exorcised from the forlorn house that is left empty, swept, and put in order. Whereupon, the restless demon travels the trackless wasteland, seeking hospitality in low places. Finding none, the fiend returns to the original haunt, only to discover the place empty. Thereupon, the demon recruits seven other spirits more wicked than itself, and together they occupy the house, declaring squatters' rights. Seven is the biblical number of perfection. Consequently, the realm of demondom has come full circle. The final verdict? The last state of that man is worse than the first. Half saved is more hazardous than unsaved.

The End of the Temple

Anglican bishop and biblical scholar, N. T. Wright, believes that Jesus' parable of the haunted house reflects a former desecration and reformation of the Jewish temple.

In 168 B.C., Syrian strongman Antiochus Epiphanies IV ordered his troops to invade Jerusalem and occupy the temple. There he erected a statue of the Greek god, Zeus, and slaughtered hogs in the Holy of Holies, an appalling rape of Jewish sensitivities. This act of blasphemy is recorded in Scripture as "the abomination of desolation" (Mark 13:14).

Eventually, Israeli freedom fighters, led by Judas Maccabeus (1 Macc. 4:36-51), drove the Syrians out of Judea, cleansed the sanctuary of its defilement, and rededicated the temple in the feast of Hanukkah during the month of December. The feast is still celebrated annually during the holiday season with the greeting, "Happy Hanukkah!"[2]

But the temple was only half saved. Like the haunted house, it was left empty, swept, and put in order. This physical and moral vacuum is eventually vulnerable to a far more sinister occupation of evil.

When Jesus appears as the fulfillment of prophecy—"and the Lord shall suddenly come to his temple" (Mal. 3:1)—he looks beyond the temple's masonry for signs of its mission to the nations. He sees only money-changers who have renovated the outer court of the Gentiles into the mammon of a merchandise mart. The house of prayer for all nations has become a den of thieves (Mark 11:17). This is the "abomination of desolation." This marks the end of temple religion. The last state of that house is worse than the first. Half saved is more hazardous than unsaved, when reformation stops short of transformation.

The Peril of Apostasy

The parable of the haunted house warns the apostolic church of the peril of apostasy. The apostle Peter, writing to the church at Rome during threatened persecution and possible defections from the faith, revisits Jesus' parable and reproduces its warning:

> For by what a man is overcome, by this he is enslaved. For if they have escaped the defilements of the world by the knowledge of the Lord and Savior Jesus Christ, they are again entangled in them and are overcome, the last state has become worse for them than the first. For it would be better for them not to have known the way of righteousness, than having known it, to turn away from the holy commandment delivered to them. (2 Pet. 2:19b-21 NASB)

Half saved is more hazardous than unsaved because the church has a poor record of reclaiming the fallen from the faith. This fact is demonstrable in the living human documents in every church.

He belonged to what news journalist Tom Brokaw has called "the best generation." Like thousands of veterans following World War II, he returned to the church and testified to a desire for change. With the finely chiseled features of a film star, a beautiful wife, and a baby on the way, he exuded an air of utter sincerity. Soon, "Mr. Clean-cut," as he was known, was given a Sunday school class of "junior boys."

From that class came several business and civic leaders, one policeman, and one preacher. The boys hung on to their teacher's every word as he alluded occasionally to his former life in the world. His influence would leave lasting memories.

But "Mr. Clean-cut" did not last. Eventually he left the church, divorced his wife, and disappeared into the moral twilight. He never came back. Years later, the boy who became a policeman was on patrol one night and stopped a motorist for speeding and wreckless driving. Shining his light on the disheveled driver, the officer demanded his driver's license. Upon reading the name on the license, the policeman was startled. "Is this really you, Mr. _____?" he asked. "Yea," the driver sadly answered, calling the policeman by his first name. "It's me." Indeed, "for by what a man is overcome, by this he is enslaved."

The former "Mr. Clean-cut," now a rumpled heap of dereliction on the side of the road amid flashing blue lights, signals another incomplete conversion. God alone knows the sincerity or status of the man's soul. One fact is obvious: the last state of that man was worse than the first.

Mary Webb wrote a poem that tells of a human love that came, and then was lost. The poem might be addressed, not to a human beloved, but to Christ by those who once walked with him but fell away.

> Why did you with strong fingers fling aside
> The gates of possibility, and say
> With vital voice the words I dream today?
> Before, I was not much unsatisfied:
> But since a god has touched me and departed,
> I run through every temple, broken-hearted.[3]

These lines portray the future of those who forsake Christ for "the narrow horizon and the tasteless tedium of an unredeemed existence."[4] Run through every temple brokenhearted, and the very stones will cry out, "You Fool!" Such is the fate of incomplete conversions.

Complete Conversion

But what is the appearance of a complete conversion? Can we discover that dynamic in the human soul that evokes the benediction, "The last state of that person is better than the first"?

Luke's Gospel compares and contrasts the incomplete conversion in the parable of the haunted house with the complete conversion in the person of Mary Magdalene: "And the twelve were with him and also some women who had been healed of evil spirits and diseases: Mary who was called Magdalene, from whom seven demons had come out, and Joanna the wife of Cuza, Herod's steward, and Susanna, and many others were contributing to their support out of their private means" (Luke 8:1b-3 NASB).

Like the haunted house, Magdalene's thralldom to evil was total, but her deliverance from evil was final. The dynamic of her deliverance is defined in the title of a famous sermon preached by Thomas Chalmers of Scotland, "The Expulsive Power of a New Affection." Jesus Christ becomes for Magdalene the expulsive power—"the devils believe and tremble" (James 2:19)—and the new incarnation of the old commandment—"You shall love the Lord your God . . ." (Deut. 6:5). While the haunted house was left empty, swept, and put in order, the haunted woman was left filled with the Spirit of Jesus—and the last state of that woman was better than the first.

This expulsive power is still demonstrable today. On November 22, 1963, when the eyes of the world were focused on President Kennedy's assassination in Dallas, Texas, C. S. Lewis died at his home in Oxford, England. The most celebrated Christian convert of the twentieth century quietly slipped away.

If C. S. Lewis had sat on a park bench at Oxford with the old tramp we met at the beginning, we might reconstruct their conversation as follows:

Tramp: You ever been saved?

Lewis: Yep, got saved at the University back in 1929. Sitting alone one night in my room, I was suddenly surprised by joy!

Tramp: What brought that on?

Lewis: For the first time I examined myself with a seriously practical purpose, and there I found what appalled me: a zoo of lusts, a bedlam of accusations, a nursery of fears, a heart of fondled hatreds. My name was Legion.[5]

Tramp: Legion? Wasn't he the fellow in the Bible who was possessed by evil spirits?

Lewis: Yes, and I was that man—a haunted house. But the Lord moved into my life as a new tenant. At first, perhaps you can't understand what he's doing. He is getting the drains right and stopping the leaks in the roof and so on; you knew these jobs needed doing, and so you are not surprised. But persistently he starts knocking the house apart in a way that hurts abominably and that doesn't seem to make sense. [Actually] he is building a different house from the one you thought of—throwing out a new wing here, putting on an extra floor there, running up towers, making courtyards. You thought you were going to be made into a decent little cottage; but he is building a palace . . . My life is his, and he plans to live there forever.[6]

Lewis' conversion was apparently a complete one, another haunted house that experienced the expulsive power of a new affection. Jesus would conclude, "The last state of that man is better than the first." The old tramp would probably say, "Mebbie ... you are saved!"

A Prayer

> Grant us, our Father, your grace, that, seeing ourselves in the light of your holiness, we may be cleansed of the pride and vainglory which obscures your truth; and knowing that from you no secrets are hid, we may perceive and confront those deceits and disguises by which we deceive ourselves and our fellowman. So may we worship you in spirit and in truth and in your light, the Light. Amen.
>
> —Reinhold Niebuhr[7]

Notes

[1]David Buttrick, *Preaching Jesus Christ* (Philadelphia: Fortress Press, 2002), 45.

[2]Garry Wills, *What Jesus Meant* (New York: Viking, Penguin Group, 2006), 74.

[3]James S. Stewart, *King Forever* (Nashville/New York: Abingdon Press, 1975), 112.

[4]Ibid. Stewart applies Webb's poem to the Apostle Paul and the biblical character Demas, who forsook Paul and Christ and "departed for Thessalonica" (2 Tim. 4:10). Stewart insists that had Demas returned to the church at Thessalonica, he would have been welcomed by the fellowship and embraced by Christ.

[5]C. S. Lewis, *Surprised by Joy* (New York/London: Harcourt, Inc., 1955), 219.

[6]Edmund A. Steimle, *Are You Looking For God? and Other Sermons* (Philadelphia: Fortress Press, 1957), 82.

[7]Reinhold Niebuhr, *Justice and Mercy*, ed. Ursula M. Niebuhr (New York: Harper & Row, 1974), 10.

CHAPTER 14

BEYOND MOCKERY ...
The Sand Against the Wind

The Lord God has given me the tongue of the learned, that I should know how to speak a word in season to him who is weary. He awakens me morning by morning, he awakens my ear to hear as the learned. The Lord God has opened my ear; and I was not rebellious, nor did I turn away. I gave my back to those who struck me, and my cheeks to those who plucked out the beard; I did not hide my face from shame and spitting.

—Isaiah 50:4-6

And the high priest stood up in the midst and asked Jesus, saying, "Do you answer nothing? What is it these men testify against you?" But he kept silent and answered nothing. Again the high priest asked him, saying to him, "Are you the Christ, the Son of the Blessed?" Jesus said, "I am. And you will see the Son of Man sitting at the right hand of the Power, and coming with the clouds of heaven." Then the high priest tore his clothes and said, "What further need do we have of witnesses? You have heard the blasphemy! What do you think?" And they all condemned him to be deserving of death. Then some began to spit on him, and to blindfold him, and to beat him, and to say to him, "Prophesy!" And the officers struck him with the palms of their hands.

—Mark 14:60-65

Where is the wise? Where is the scribe? Where is the disputer of this age? Has not God made foolish the wisdom of this world? For since, in the wisdom of God, the world through wisdom did not know God, it pleased God through the foolishness of the message preached to save those who believe.

—1 Corinthians 1:20-21

If patriotism is the "last refuge of a scoundrel,"[1] then ridicule is the last refuge of an unbeliever. The mockery of the messenger of God—and the message—is the final defense against the truth. The kingdom of heaven is like an invitation to a royal wedding, according to Jesus' parable (Matt. 22:1-5), but the recipients "made light of it." But to make light of the truth in no way diminishes the weight of truth.

When the French skeptic Voltaire lay on his deathbed, a priest was summoned to administer the last rites: "Voltaire, do you hereby renounce the devil and all his works?" "Padre," he pleaded, "This is no time to be making enemies!"[2]

Thus Voltaire died as he lived—in levity and mockery. His influence on his times would inspire a volume of history written by Will and Ariel Durant, *The Age of Voltaire*. But his memory would evoke some lines of poetry.

In his private papers, the English poet William Blake penned a message to Voltaire and all who join him in the ridicule of things holy:

> Mock on, Mock on, Voltaire (and company)…
> Mock on, Mock on, 'tis all in vain.
> You throw the sand against the wind,
> And the wind blows it back again.[3]

These lines confront us with the vanity—and futility—of mockery.

Jesus Christ: Prophet, Priest, and King

On Good Friday, the city of Jerusalem is filled with "loud mockers in the roaring street[s]."[4] By day's end, Christ's trinity of sacred offices—prophet, priest, and king—will be buried beneath the rubble of ridicule, and his body buried in a borrowed grave.

At the scene of crucifixion during his hour of dereliction, wagging tongues mock Christ's priestly intersession: "Ha! He saved others, but he cannot save himself" (Mark 15:31).

In the Roman barracks, bawdy soldiers callously mock Jesus' claim to kingship: "And they dressed him in purple, and after weaving a crown of thorns, they put it on him; and they began to proclaim him, 'Hail king of the Jews!'" (Mark 15:17-18 NASB). The rapier of their ridicule must have cut as deeply into his sensitive spirit as their subsequent flagellation would cut into his naked flesh (Mark 15:15).

In the judgment hall of the Sanhedrin, Israel's highest tribunal, the high priest and justices force Jesus to preach a "trial sermon" to expose him as a false prophet. They play a children's game, "Blindman's Bluff," where a player is blindfolded and tries to find others while being hit with husks of papyrus. "And some began to spit at him and to blindfold him and to beat him with their fists, and say to him 'Prophesy!'" (Mark 14:65 NASB).

This child's game played with adult cruelty makes a burlesque of Jesus' ability to prophesy.[5] His preaching is treated with the seriousness of a vulgar vaudeville comedy, as his royalty is reduced to the level of a sleazy act of striptease.

The scene in the judgment hall closes. The "trial sermon" is over. Security men take Jesus into custody with slaps in the face, an ironic footnote to the fulfillment of prophecy: "I did not hide my face from shame and spitting" (Isa. 50:6) and "they hated me without a cause" (Ps. 35:19). The hateful exposure of the false prophet has simply confirmed the true prophet:

> Mock on, Mock on, High Priest . . .
> Mock on, Mock on, Sanhedrin . . .
> 'Tis all in vain!
> . . . Sand against the wind!

The Habitat of Hate

A slap in the face is the most humiliating, hateful, and contradictory form of interrogation. In the judgment hall, men desperately—and even violently—seek the truth they passionately hate and adamantly reject.

Mark's scene parallels an episode recorded by the historian in a theatre of war (1 Kings 22). King Ahab of Israel plans to attack the border town of Ramoth-Gilead. Desperate to know the mind of God, he convenes a conference on biblical prophecy. Four hundred royal court chaplains supported by the state gather to seek not the mind of God, but the mind of Ahab and to prophesy what he wants to hear: "Go up, for the Lord will deliver it into the hand of the king" (1 Kings 22:6). The lying prophets may not know the mind of God, but they remember who pays their salaries.

But cautious Jehoshaphat calls for a second opinion: "Is there not still a prophet of the Lord here, that we may inquire of him?" (1 Kings 22:7). Ahab replies, "There is . . . Micaiah, the son of Imlah . . . but I hate him, because he does not prophesy good concerning me, but evil" (1 Kings 22:8).

However, prodded by public pressure, Ahab reluctantly summons Micaiah from prison and swears him to "tell the truth, the whole truth, and nothing but the truth." Under oath, the prophet of the Lord reports a vision of the aftermath of battle at Ramoth-Gilead: "I saw all Israel scattered on the mountains, as sheep without a shepherd" (who has died in battle). Irate, Ahab exclaims: "Did I not tell you he would not prophesy good concerning me, but evil?" (1 Kings 22:18). Whereupon Zedekiah, one of the prophetic hirelings, walks over and slaps the man of God across the cheek (1 Kings 22:24). The point of this story? The leader of the nation will die because he will not hear the truth from a prophet he hates.[6]

Similarly, Mark portrays in the judgment hall the leaders of the nation—the high priest, Caiphas, and the judges of the court—who will die because they will not hear the truth from the prophet they hate.

Consequently, the preaching life exists—and endures—in the habitat of hate. Another word for the habitat is the world. Hate is the essence of the world, just as love is the essence of Christ. Therefore, the world is opposed to Christ and hates all who articulate his truth. The apostle John cautions especially preachers and missionaries not "to be surprised if the world hates you" (1 John 3:13).

On the day before Christmas Eve of 2011 in New Orleans, a young minister and his support group conducted a worship service on Bourbon Street. They sang of faraway Bethlehem in the lovely carols, and preached the wonders of the Prince of Peace. But the crowd turned surly and ugly: "For hate is strong and mocks the song of peace on earth; good will to men." Suddenly, a middle-aged, intoxicated woman walked over and slapped the preacher and cursed the group: "You're all a bunch of liars!" The young people expressed puzzlement that hatred for Jesus is so palpable.[7] But Jesus predicted such experiences and prepared his own followers: "If the world hates you, it hated me before it hated you" (John 15:18).

Today, the preaching office appears to be in disrepair. Deans of divinity schools and professors of homiletics lament the lack of candidates for the pulpit and the loss of the craft of preaching.

Nevertheless, an apostolic absolute is given to the fraternity of preaching and the listening community: "It pleased God through the foolishness of preaching to save those who believe" (1 Cor. 1:21). That divine felicity apparently includes even the foolishness of the preacher.

The Foolishness of Preaching

To be sure, the listening community—the church—has endured more than its share of preachers who make the gospel of a crucified God more foolish than it already is. Speaking for Protestants, President Woodrow Wilson, son of a Presbyterian pastor, wrote, "One of the proofs of the divinity of our religion is the preaching it has survived."[8]

Speaking for Catholics, the late Senator Daniel P. Moynihan wrote: "In some fifteen years of listening seriously I do not believe I have more than once or twice heard an interesting idea delivered from the pulpit of an American Catholic Church . . . by and large the homilies . . . are an affront to taste as well as intelligence . . . protest is in order."[9]

However, the apostle Paul, having pondered the venal motives and the sloppy methods of some preachers, came to an entirely different conclusion and conviction: "Some are preaching Christ even from envy and strife, but some from good will; [others] out of selfish ambition, rather than pure motives . . . What then? Only that in every way, whether in pretense or truth Christ is preached . . . and I rejoice" (Phil. 1:15-18 NASB).

Rejoice when Christ is preached in pretense? Yes, even in pretense. The message of the gospel of God will transcend the motives—and even the mockery—of some messengers. Fred Craddock, professor of preaching at Emory University, once tried to put some confidence back into preachers by restoring some confidence in their gospel.

He told of a visit of theologian Marcus Barth to the University of Texas at Austin during the annual talent night. There, fraternities and sororities compete for the prize, "Best Talent." One fraternity, the "Animal House" crowd, decided to put on a mock revival meeting. They elected a preacher, formed a choir, and practiced singing "Amazing Grace."

Their dress rehearsal was held on Saturday morning in an empty auditorium, except for a lone custodian painting in the back of the building. The preacher gave a rousing performance: "Repent! Turn to Jesus! Come on down to the front and get saved while there is still time!"

His pleas were accompanied by the plaintive sounds of the choir singing "Just as I Am":

> Just as I am, without one plea,
> But that Thy blood was shed for me,
> And that Thou bidd'st me come to Thee,
> O Lamb of God, I come, I come.

The "revival" ended with spirits high and the slapping of high fives; surely such a performance would bring the house down and win the first prize. But the group's euphoria was penetrated by a moment of gravity: The lone custodian who had been painting in the back of the building suddenly appeared on his profession of faith.[10] Indeed, it pleased God through the foolishness of preaching—and even the pretense of the preacher—to save those who believe.

> Mock on, Mock on animal house,
> Mock on sorority sisters, 'Tis all in vain.
> You throw the sand against the wind,
> And the wind blows it back again.

The mockery of God across the ages has managed to establish but one fact: God is not mocked (Gal. 6:7).

A Prayer

> Almighty God, who has placed us in a world of things true and false, noble and base; grant us clearness of vision and sure judgment wherever good is intertwined with evil and duty conflicts with desire, and at all hours a settled purpose of seeking thy will and the things that endure, and of living in the joy of thy glorious and eternal kingdom. Amen.
>
> —Hugh Cameron[11]

Notes

[1]Samuel Johnson, publisher of the first English dictionary, defined patriotism as the "last refuge of a scoundrel."

[2]This story may be apocryphal. For a fuller treatment on Voltaire's agnosticism, see Canon Henry Lewis' volume, *Modern Rationalism as Seen at Work in Its Biographies* (London: Society for Promoting Christian Knowledge, 1913), 10-43.

[3]*The Oxford Dictionary of Quotations*, ed. Elizabeth Knowles (Oxford: Oxford University Press, 1999), 120.

[4]James Stewart, *A Faith to Proclaim* (New York: Charles Scribner's Sons, 1953), 116.

[5]Raymond E. Brown, *The Death of the Messiah* (New York: Doubleday, 1999), 575.

[6]Richard Nelson, *First and Second Kings*, Interpretation: A Bible Commentary for Teaching and Preaching (Louisville: John Knox Press, 1987), 151.

[7]http://heismydelight.wordpress.com/2011/12/25/the-eve-of-christmas-eve-on-bourbon-street-new-orleans/

[8]*Best Sermons*, ed. G. Paul Butler, vol. 10 (New York: Trident Press, 2007), 12.

[9]Ibid.

[10]Fred Craddock related this event at a conference on preaching in the 1990s at Briarlake Baptist Church in Decatur, Georgia.

[11]*Prayers for Services*, ed. Morgan Phelps Noyes (New York: Scribner's Sons, 1945), 97.

CHAPTER 15

BEYOND THE LIE ...
What Is Truth?

John 18:33-38a

Today we are a nation of relativists for whom there are no enduring truths, let alone any that are self-evident.

—*Allan Bloom*[1]

In his compelling and controversial film, *The Passion of the Christ*, Mel Gibson devotes some fifteen harrowing minutes to the trial of Jesus Christ before the Roman governor, Pontius Pilate. Jesus is accused of the twin capital crimes of religious blasphemy and political heresy: He claims to be God, and he claims to be a king.

Pilate begins the proceedings with the political question, "Are you the King of the Jews?" (John 18:33c). Jesus reassures the Roman that his kingdom poses no political or military threat to Rome: "My kingdom is not of this world" (John 18:36a). The kingdom of God appears from neither the religious right nor the liberal left, but from the realm beyond.

Furthermore, the prisoner declares both his mission and vocation: "For this cause I was born and for this cause I have come into the world to bear witness to the truth. Everyone who is of the truth hears my voice" (John 18:37).

Pilate's reply is probably meant to be cynical: "What is truth?" (John 18:38).

Mel Gibson, perhaps more sympathetic to the Roman governor than the evangelist, makes Pilate say: "You have your truth, and I have my truth." That sentence is not written in the Gospel text, but it is written in the texture of the American character. In that one sentence—"You have your truth, and I have my truth"—Mel Gibson reflects the sign of the times, the spirit of the age. The only absolute? There are no absolutes! The modest claim of "You have your truth, and I have my truth" has become an evasion of truth.

In such a climate of "truth decay" we are wise to compare and contrast the truth of Jesus Christ according to the Gospel of John with the truth of Pontias Pilate according to Mel Gibson.

Jesus Christ: Truth through Personality

Both Jesus' origin and destiny are bound up in his mission and message: "to bear witness to the truth." Both the message and the man are inseparable: "and the word became flesh" (John 1:14a).

Thus Phillips Brooks defined the role of the fraternity of preaching as "truth through personality."[2] The witness from God requires both. The truth of the message is fixed and final; the truth of the personality is dynamic—unfolding through the preacher's character, affections, and every fiber of moral being. Both "preaching and personality are inextricably intertwined."[3]

The message of truth may attract and repel. Following Jesus' mission in Galilee and his message about the cross, "many of his disciples withdrew, and were walking with him no more" (John 6:66). Turning to the twelve, Jesus asks, "You do not want to go away also, do you?" In his finest hour, Peter asks, "Lord, to whom shall we go? You have the words of eternal life" (John 6:67-68). Truth and personality are indeed inextricably intertwined.

Perhaps the most distinctive dimension of human personality is the speaking voice—words of eternal life! During the days of silent films in Hollywood, careers and fortunes were made by actors who projected their presence on the screen, their words in silent captions beneath. But with the advent of the "talkies," many careers were ruined because their presence on the screen lacked the persuasion of the speaking voice. The voice makes or unmakes personality.

Furthermore, the authority of the message is conveyed in the speaking voice. Therefore, when the temple police, sent by the chief priests and Pharisees to arrest Jesus, returned empty-handed, they explained, "Never did a man speak the way this man speaks" (John 7:46). Men and women still listen for his voice, because faith comes by hearing.

By the year 1885, Thomas Edison had perfected the phonograph. People came from all over the world to East Orange, New Jersey, to listen to the recorded sounds of the human voice, the most beautiful of that time belonging to the Swedish nightingale, Jenny Lind. Henry Stanley, the London journalist who had found David Livingstone in Africa, interviewed Edison about his phonograph. Stanley, a believer, asked Edison, a life-long agnostic: "Mr. Edison, if it were possible for you to hear the voice of any man . . . known in the history of the world, whose voice would you prefer to hear?" "Napoleon's," replied Edison without hesitation. Stanley said, "No, no, I should like to hear the voice of our Savior." "Oh well," laughed Edison, "You know I like a hustler!"[4]

The Gospel according to John is our phonograph. We listen for the voice of Jesus from its pages: "If you continue in my word . . . you shall know the truth, and the truth will make you free" (John 8:31b-32). This freedom is born of truth delivered through Jesus Christ the Living Word (personality) who breathes on the written word (truth).

Pontius Pilate: The Futility of Neutrality

What is the role of the Roman governor in the drama of Good Friday? If Jesus Christ reveals the truth of reality, expressed through personality, Pontius Pilate exposes the futility of neutrality. "He who is not with me," says Jesus, "is against me; and he who does not gather with me scatters" (Matt. 12:30). Indubitably true! But once the truth is said, it will then be believed or denied; but it will not be ignored.

Barbara Brown Taylor, the distinguished Episcopal author and preacher, tells of the Alaska hunter who was visited one day by the local missionary. "Padre," the hunter said, "I've been meaning to ask you a question. If you had not come to our village years ago and told us about God and sin, would I go to hell?" "Why surely not," said the missionary. "We are only accountable for the truth we have been given." "Then, Padre," replied the hunter, "why in the world did you have to come and tell us?"[5]

The old hunter sensed that once the truth is spoken, the freedom to choose does not accommodate the freedom not to choose.

Edwin Markham, the poet, heard God say:

I will leave man to make the fatal guess,
Will leave him torn between the No and the Yes,
Leave him unresting till he rests in Me,
Drawn upward by the choice that makes him free
Leave him in tragic loneliness to choose,
With all in life to win or all to lose.[6]

That is how the Gospel story leaves Pontius Pilate—torn between "the No and the Yes". This political hack cannot bring himself to say either. The drama ends with the pathetic sacrament of neutrality.

In the upper room, Jesus had girded himself with a towel, and with a basin of water washed the disciples' feet—symbolic of humility. Outside the judgment hall, Pilate orders a basin of water in which to dip his hands—symbolic of neutrality. There, like Lady Macbeth who shouted, "Out, out, damned spot," he tries to wash from his hands the blood of an innocent man. "I'm innocent of the blood of this just person. You see to it" (Matt. 27: 24).

And yet, every Sunday for twenty centuries, Christians have stood and repeated those familiar words of the Apostles Creed: "I believe in Jesus Christ . . . suffered under Pontius Pilate . . . Crucified, dead . . . buried . . ."

Neutrality is the refuge of a coward.

The Truth of Jesus Christ Prevails

In his acceptance speech for the Nobel Prize for Literature, Alexander Solzhenitsyn left the world a legacy of hope: "One word of truth outweighs the whole world."[7]

You may nail the truth to a tree; cut it down and embalm it with spices; give it a funeral fit for a pharaoh; seal the grave with imperial authority; surround it with a bodyguard of lies. But on the third day it will rise again, and the church will echo the words of "The Battle Hymn of the Republic": "His truth is marching on. Glory, Hallelujah!"

John Masefield, in his play, *The Trial of Jesus*, penned an epilogue to the question, "What is truth?" The only witness who speaks up for Jesus at his trial is Pilate's wife, Lady Claudia Procula. During the trial she sends her husband an urgent message imploring him to "have nothing to do with that just man" (Matt. 27:19). Upon hearing that Jesus is crucified, she finds the Roman centurion who supervised the execution and asks, "Do you think he's dead?" "No Lady, I don't," he answers. The conversation continues: "Then, where is he?" "Let loose in the world, Lady, where neither Jew nor Roman can stop his truth."[8]

A Prayer

> God, defend us, not against the truth which reveals to us our true being and motives, character and purposes; but against the lie which misrepresents and misjudges. So give us patience to bear with those who will not understand when we speak in good will; and resolution not to be moved whereby weakness, integrity, and goodness would be compromised. For his sake we pray, who was the truth slain by the lie, who, being reviled, reviled not again, remaining steadfast to the end. Amen.
>
> —John McIntyre[9]

Notes

[1]Quoted by David F. Wells in *Above All Earthly Powers: Christ in a Postmodern World* (Grand Rapids: Wm. B. Eerdmans Publishing Co., 2005), 85.

[2]Phillips Brooks, *Eight Lectures on Preaching* (London: S.P.C.K., 1959), 28.

[3]Batsell Barrett Baxter, *The Heart of the Yale Lectures* (New York: Macmillan Co., 1947), 18-19.

[4]Matthew Josephson, *Edison: A Biography* (New York: Francis Parkman Prize Edition History Book Club, 1959), 323.

[5]Barbara Brown Taylor, *Speaking of Sin: The Lost Language of Salvation* (Cambridge, MA: Cowley Publications, 2001), 41.

[6]Edwin Markham, "Man-Test," *Poems of Edwin Markham* (New York: Harper & Brothers, 1950), 56.

[7]John R. W. Scott, *Between Two Worlds: The Art of Preaching in the Twentieth Century* (Grand Rapids: Wm. B. Erdmanns Publishing, 1982), 105.

[8]John Frederick Jansen, *No Idle Tale* (Richmond, VA: John Knox Press, 1967), 62.

[9]John McIntyre, *Theology After the Storm* (Grand Rapids: Wm. B. Eerdmans Publishing, 1997), 257.

CHAPTER 16

BEYOND DESPAIR ...
The Word Became Tears

Genesis 50:24; Luke 19:41-42, 44b

How lonely sits the city
That was full of people!
How like a widow is she,
Who was great among the nations!
The princess among the provinces
Has become a slave!

She weeps bitterly in the night,
Her tears are on her cheeks;
Among all her lovers
She has none to comfort her.
All her friends have dealt treacherously with her;
They have become her enemies.

Judah has gone into captivity,
Under affliction and hard servitude;
She dwells among the nations,
She finds no rest;
All her persecutors overtake her in dire straits.

Is it nothing to you, all you who pass by?
Behold and see
If there is any sorrow like my sorrow,
Which has been brought on me,
Which the LORD has inflicted
In the day of his fierce anger.

—Lamentations 1:1-3, 12

You did not recognize the time of your visitation.

—Luke 19:44c

Some of you may remember Governor Adlai Stevenson of Illinois. He twice lost the race for the American presidency to the popular war hero, General Dwight Eisenhower. The story is told that, following his loss by a landslide, someone asked the governor, "How does it feel to lose the greatest political prize?" He replied: "I feel like the boy who stubbed his toe; I'm too big to cry, and it hurts too much to laugh."

But Jesus Christ, the strong Son of God, "The Lion of the tribe of Judah" (Rev. 5:5), was not too big to cry, and he often hurt too much to laugh. At the grave of Lazarus his friend, his love evoked the shortest, but one of the most profound verses in the Bible: "Jesus wept" (John 11:35).

When he saw the city of Jerusalem for the last time, he was convulsed with sobs, and lamented, "If only you had known the things that make for peace! But now they are hidden from your eyes . . . because you did not recognize the time of your visitation" (Luke 19:42, 44 NASB). At Jesus' birth the Word became flesh (John 1:14); at his death the Word became tears. But the tears will prevail! "For his anger is but for a moment, his favor is for life; weeping may endure for a night, but joy comes in the morning" (Ps. 30:5).

Once to Every Man and Nation

Perhaps no preacher has portrayed the poignancy of divine sorrow as the Anglican, F. W. Robertson. Robertson's preaching ignited a candle that burned brightly but briefly above the resort town of Brighton, England. But he died at the age of thirty-seven. Fortunately, some women in the congregation knew shorthand and transcribed some of his sermons for posterity.

In his assessment of the scene of Christ weeping for Jerusalem, Robertson offered a sweeping surgical analysis of the text that defies improvement. Said he, three times come to every person and nation: a time of grace, a time of blindness, and a time of judgment. For Jerusalem, it is the time of blindness. The time of grace is already past; the time of judgment is yet to come.[1]

Alas! The citizens of the city could read the signs of the weather, but they could not read the signs of the times (Matt. 16:3). The sight of such blindness left Jesus in tears.

The visitations of God can almost always be traced in a trail of tears. All roads may lead to Rome, but the trail of tears leads to Jerusalem, the graveyard of prophecy: "O, Jerusalem, Jerusalem, the city that kills the prophets, and stones those sent to her!" (Luke 13:34 NASB). Every visitation of God evokes rejection of the messenger, regardless of the mood or medium of the message:

• Jeremiah comes weeping, his eyes a fountain of tears—and he is dumped into a pit (Jer. 38:12-13).
• Isaiah comes reasoning and regal, "Come now, let us reason together"—and he is sawn asunder.[2]
• Zechariah, filled with the Spirit, comes worshipping—and he is stoned to death near the high alter (2 Chron. 24:21).
• John the Baptist comes preaching, "a burning and a shining light"—and he is beheaded (John 5:33-35).
• Finally Jesus appears in the fullness of time, born of a woman, King of the Jews—and the people declare: "We do not want this man to reign over us" (Luke 19:14 NASB).

The Strife of Truth with Falsehood

Why do truth-tellers evoke such resistance and rejection within the human community? Why is Jerusalem the graveyard of prophecy?

Historian R. G. Collingwood believes that the community's rejection of prophets is attributed to the nature of prophecy itself. He includes all inspired artists as prophets, and all prophets as artists, because they painstakingly toil over their message, whatever their particular medium: the preacher with her Bible, the painter with his oils and canvas, the sculptor with his clay, the poet with her verses, the music man with his "Halleluiah Chorus"—all prophecy.

Furthermore, to prophesy is not to foretell the future. To prophesy, according to Collingwood, "is to tell the audience, at the risk of their displeasure, the secrets of their own hearts."[2] "The heart is deceitful above all things and desperately wicked. Who can know it?" (Jer. 17:9).

The prophet knows it. Therefore, the audience needs prophets because they reveal, not their own secrets, but those of the audience. Without the prophet, the human community deceives itself on the one subject concerning which ignorance means death: the corruption of consciousness.[3] And what is that corruption? Jesus traced it to the evil thoughts nursed within the human heart: "murders, adulteries, fornications, false witness, and slanders. These are the things which defile the man" (Matt. 15:19-20 NASB). And the remedy for this ignorance, this corruption? The medicine is contained in the prophet's message: the sermon, the psalm, the painting, the novel, the symphony.

Before his death, Henri Nouwen, beloved priest and author, flew to St. Petersburg, Russia, to visit the Hermitage Museum. Strangely compelled by a reprint of a Rembrandt painting, *The Return of the Prodigal Son*, Nouwen sat for days transfixed before the original huge canvas. On one side stands the father, his arms flung around the shoulders of the ragged boy; on the other side stands the elder brother, splendidly attired, wearing gold rings, elegant but sullen, angry, and unforgiving (Luke 15). Nouwen suddenly saw himself in the painting. He was the elder brother! The firstborn child, Henri never disobeyed his father's commands; dutifully entering the priesthood, he never disobeyed his superior's orders. But like the elder brother in the parable, Henri found himself filled with anger and resentment; overly sensitive to criticism; guilty not of the sins of the flesh, but the sins of disposition.[4]

As a priest, Nouwen had read the parable of the prodigal son and elder brother numerous times, but for the first time the parable read him. And the parable's message contains the medicine: God loves angry, elder brothers—and receives them! But some refuse the medicine. The prophecy that exposes the secrets of the audience must risk the displeasure of the audience. The hearers may rise up and declare to the prophet, "We would rather be ruined than changed."[5] The word is denial.

Yet the Truth Alone Is Strong

Old Testament scholar Kathleen O'Connor confesses that Lamentations became her biblical companion, not to advance her career but to save her very self. She grew up in a loving family that practiced denial. Anger was forbidden, sorrow was ignored, and hard things were silenced. She said, "We practiced denial: we looked on the bright side, walked on the sunny side, and remembered that tomorrow is another day . . . deaths went ungrieved, anger lurked but could not speak, and broken dreams were barely noticed." And what were the results of this denial? "Some of us," she concluded, "lost great chunks of ourselves in the process."[6] No wonder she read Lamentations to recover herself.

Therefore, lament denies denial; lament is a form of truth-telling; lament remains love's last appeal. Tears sometimes go on pleading long after words have fallen silent and argument has rested its case.

By the time of Luke's Gospel, Jesus' future prophecy of judgment has been fulfilled. Jerusalem the Golden has become Ground Zero. Not one stone is left on top of another, but with one exception: the Wailing Wall of King Herod's temple remains as a monument to the Master's tears. There pilgrims gather each day to pray, worship, and weep. "The chiefest sanctity of a temple," wrote Unamuno, "is that it is a place to which men and women go to weep in common . . . it is not enough to cure the plague; we must learn to weep over it."[7]

The Wailing Wall remains an historic footnote to a former house of prayer whose mission was committed to all nations.

Theologian C. S. Song tells a Chinese parable about the power of tears. A young couple was separated on their wedding day by soldiers who forced Lady Meng's new husband to join the laborers building China's Great Wall. Like many others, the husband never returned. Strong men went in search of the lost laborers and failed to find them or their remains. But when Lady Meng stood before the wall, her tears alone were strong enough to cause the wall's collapse and to reveal the bones of the dead who built it.[8]

Lady Meng's tears expressed personal sorrow and political resistance. Her public lament unsettled the world's wicked arrangements, revealed rulers' dark secrets, and exposed the bones of the enslaved. The power of a woman's tears exposed the cover-up of corrupt men. Lament, indeed, is love's last appeal and truth's final testimony.

The compassionate Christ who weeps for the city remains the great physician who visits his people. Soon during the days of his flesh he will be raised on a cross "with healing in his wings" (Mal. 4:2). If we are wise, we shall pray daily for discernment to recognize the time of our visitation.

Three times, just three times, said the Brighton preacher, come to every person and nation: a time of grace, a time of blindness, and a time of judgment. For Jerusalem, it was the time of blindness. And Jesus wept. I wonder what time it is for us.

A Prayer

Keep watch, dear Lord, with those who work, or watch, or weep this night, and give your angels charge over those who sleep. Tend the sick, Lord Christ; give rest to the weary, bless the dying, soothe the suffering, pity the afflicted, shield the joyous; and all for your love's sake. Amen.

—*The Book of Common Prayer*

Notes

[1] Robertson's summary of Christ weeping for the city was quoted years ago in a volume no longer available. The craft of his preaching and representative sermons from his brief ministry are found in *The Preaching of F. W. Robertson*, ed. Gilbert E. Doan, Jr. (Philadelphia: Fortress Press, 1964).

[2] R. E. C. Browne, *The Ministry of the Word* (Philadelphia: Fortress Press, 1976), 20.

[3] Ibid.

[4] Henri J. M. Nouwen, *The Return of the Prodigal Son* (New York: Image Books Doubleday, 1992), 69.

[5] W. H. Auden, http://quote.robertgenn.com.

[6] Kathleen M. O'Connor, *Lamentations & the Tears of the World* (Maryknoll, NY: Orbis Books, 2002), 89.

[7] Miguel De Unamuno, *Tragic Sense of Life* (New York: Dover Publications, 1954), 17.

[8] O'Connor, 130.

CHAPTER 17

BEYOND THE SILENCE ...
Hush! Somebody's Calling My Name!

John 20:1-18

What word so explosive as that one Palestinian word with the endlessness of its fallout?

—*David Catchpole*[1]

The township of Greer, South Carolina, numbers some 20,000 souls. But at the city limits the welcome sign records no population census, only the name of one citizen:

> Welcome to Greer, South Carolina
> Home of Danielle Davis
> Miss South Carolina 1994

That sign is a window of the community in which the city fathers have figuratively placed the lovely face of Miss South Carolina—the representative person of a proud community.

Similarly, the empty tomb in Jerusalem, from which Christ was raised from the dead, becomes the welcome center of the resurrection community. There, the Gospel of John creates a window in which is placed the face of a special woman, Mary Magdalene, the first person to experience the resurrection faith.

The experience is framed at the beginning with the lament, "They have taken away the Lord," and ends with ecstasy, "I have seen the Lord!"

Not all Easter people experience the Easter faith in the same way or through the same sense. For Mary Magdalene, the faith is kindled not by the sense of sight (she first sees the risen Lord but does not recognize him), but by the sense of sound—the sound of Christ calling her name, "Mary!" Whereupon she exclaims, "Rabboni (Teacher)!" The old spiritual captures the gravity of the call in a moment of time:

> Hush! Somebody's calling my name.
> Hush! Somebody's calling my name.
> O my Lord, what shall I do?
> Somebody's calling my name.

What shall Magdalene do? She shall become the representative woman of the resurrection community. Hers will become the voice of the Easter people: "Go to my brethren, and say to them, 'I ascend to my Father and your Father, and to my God and your God'" (John 20:17b).

But will a court of Jewish men believe her report? Two male voices contend against her credibility: Moses' law of evidence—"By the mouth of two or three witnesses shall the matter be established" (Deut. 19:15b)—and Josephus and his gender bias—"From women let no evidence be accepted, because of the levity and temerity of their sex" (Antiquities 4:219).[2] And yet, the fallout of the Palestinian word—or name (Mary)—has demolished gender landmarks. The resurrection has relocated the role of women:

> Welcome to the Resurrection Community
> Home of Mary Magdalene
> First in the Resurrection Faith, 33 A.D.

"There is neither Jew nor Greek, there is neither slave nor free, there is neither male nor female; for you are all one in Christ Jesus" (Gal. 3:28). The representative woman speaks up for men and women who hear—and believe—the voice of the Good Shepherd.

Christ's call to Magdalene by name at the empty tomb applies a previous prophecy of Jesus on the role of the Good Shepherd delivered in the precincts of the Jewish temple: "To [the Good Shepherd] the doorkeeper opens; and the sheep hear his voice; and he calls his own sheep by name, and leads them out . . . and the sheep follow him because they know his voice" (John 10:3-4). The relationship between the sheep and the Shepherd is characterized by intimacy and affection.

The story is told that during a national census a case worker asked a struggling mother in a dingy flat, "How many children do you have?" "Well," she replied, "there's John and Thomas and Elizabeth and . . ." "I don't need their names," he interrupted, "just their number." "But sir," said she, "they are not numbers but names—and they mean everything to me."[3]

The Good Shepherd calls his own sheep by name, and they mean everything to him. And his call means everything to those who hear his voice.

"When E. F. Hutton speaks," according to the advertisement, "everyone listens." But when the Good Shepherd speaks, not everyone listens—only those who believe and belong.

"If you are the Christ, tell us plainly," challenges Christ's enemies who are plotting his death.

His answer is plain enough: "I told you and you do not believe because you are not of my sheep" (John 10:25).

To whom—besides E. F. Hutton and the Good Shepherd— do people listen? In the postmodern culture, many men and women approach the sacred through the self in search of the god within. The result: they no longer need religious institutions such as churches or synagogues; they are no longer belongers to anyone but themselves.

Perhaps the poster child of the postmodernist is portrayed in Robert Bella's interview with the young nurse, Shelia Larson: "Do you consider yourself a religious person?" "I believe in God. I'm not a religious fanatic. I can't remember the last time I went to church. My faith has carried me a long way." "How would you define your faith?" "It's Sheliaism. Just my own little voice . . . It's just try to love yourself and be gentle with yourself."[4] Sheilia Larson's religion is rooted in an effort to transform external authority into internal meaning—"my own little voice."[5]

Ibsen portrays a person of a similar faith whose creed is "Be Myself." Upon visiting a lunatic asylum, he assumes that all the patients are "outside themselves." The director corrects him:

> Outside themselves? Oh, no, you're wrong. It's here that
> men and women are most themselves—themselves and
> nothing but themselves—sailing with outspread sails
> of self. Each shuts himself in a cask of self, the cask
> stopped with a bung of self and seasoned in a well of

self. None has a tear for others' woes or cares what any other thinks. We are ourselves in thought and voice— ourselves up to the very limit; and consequently, if we want an emperor, it's very clear that you're the man.[6]

Self-centeredness is a form of lunacy. But there is another voice, a higher calling, a voice from beyond ourselves, that calls us out of ourselves, that knows us better than ourselves: the voice of the Good Shepherd. Mary Magdalene speaks for all men and women who hear and believe that voice.

The voice of Jesus, Galilean and provincial, nevertheless, transcends continents, centuries, and cultures.

"And I have other sheep who are not of the fold," prophesies the Good Shepherd, "and I must bring them also, and they shall hear my voice, and they shall become one flock with one shepherd" (John 10:17). That one flock includes the Gentile, the foreigner, the stranger—and the woman.

At times the Good Shepherd calls through a familiar text of Scripture that, because of some circumstance, sounds intensely personal.

Winifred Holtby, England's gifted novelist, in a time of profound grief—like Mary Magdalene—heard the voice of the Good Shepherd. During a routine medical exam a physician told Winifred that she had but two years to live. She was only thirty-three years of age. The season was early spring. Her home was the English sheep country. In shock over the medical verdict, Winifred went for a long walk over a hillside and stood by a trough of frozen water, surrounded by a flock of lambs unable to drink. Dejected, bitter, and rebelling angrily against her medical sentence, she broke the ice with her walking cane, whereupon she heard a voice repeat the familiar Pauline text: "Having nothing, yet possessing all things" (2 Cor. 6:10).[7]

The voice was so distinct that she looked around, startled to find herself alone with the lambs on an empty hillside: "Where one heard noise and one saw flame, I only knew he named my name."[8]

Suddenly, in a flash, the grief, the bitterness disappeared. She gamboled down the hillside with a feeling of sheer exhilaration. At that moment Winifred was called into that universal flock with one Shepherd. She lived another four years and wrote the great English novel, *South Riding*.[9] Winifred Holtby became another representative voice of the Easter people.

Therefore, we still sing "Jesus Is Tenderly Calling"—and he is. To be sure, he calls at times when we are not listening and in ways we have yet to recognize as speech.

Nicodemus, the elder scholar, heard a sound no louder than a whisper through the mysterious voice of the night wind, blowing dried leaves across the empty cobblestone streets of the sleeping city of Jerusalem, with intimations of a land of beginning again (John 3:8).

Similarly, preacher-novelist Frederick Buechner was asked by a caustic relative: "Frederick, I understand you are going into the ministry. Is this your idea, or have you been poorly advised?" It was neither. His call was no louder than the "clickety-clack" of two apple branches bumping together by a soft breeze in a New England orchard.[10] He did not try and explain to her his call. Those who have never heard would not understand.

As it did to Winifred Holtby, life may plunge us into the depths, or lift us toward the heights where a familiar verse of Scripture grabs us by the lapels and declares: "I'm talking to you; listen up!"

Therefore, God is still speaking, but at times when we are not listening and in tones we do not recognize. In the old biblical story, the boy Samuel is awakened by the whisper of his name in the dead of night. Believing the voice to belong to the elder prophet and mentor, Eli, he is wisely told: "Go, lie down; and it shall be, if he calls you, that you must say, 'Speak, LORD, for your servant hears'" (1 Sam. 3:9).

The resurrection faith is still kindled in close proximity to the listening ear. Therefore, be still. Listen. Hush! Maybe even now, somebody's calling your name!

A Prayer

> Lord, teach me to listen. The times are noisy and my ears are weary with the thousand raucous sounds which continuously assault them. Give me the spirit of the boy Samuel when he said to Thee, "Speak, for Thy servant heareth." Let me hear Thee speaking in my heart. Let me get used to the sound of Thy voice, that its tones may be familiar when the sounds of earth die away and the only sound will be the music of Thy speaking voice. Amen.
>
> —A. W. Tozer[11]

Notes

[1]David Catchpole, *Resurrection People* (Macon, GA: Smyth & Helwys Publishing, 2002), 30.

[2]Ibid., 150.

[3]The source of this story was the late Gerald Kennedy, Methodist bishop of the Los Angeles Conference. Bishop Kennedy is still remembered for his lectures to pastors at Furman University in Greenville, South Carolina.

[4]Robert N. Bellah et. al., *Habits of the Heart: Individualism and Commitment in American Life* (New York: Harper & Row, 1985), 221.

[5]Ibid., 235.

[6]George A. Buttrick, *Prayer* (New York: Abingdon Press, 1942), 37.

[7]Leslie D. Weatherhead, *Over His Own Signature* (New York: Abingdon Press, 1956), 52-53.

[8]*Rufus Jones Speaks to Our Time*, ed. Harry Emerson Fosdick (New York: Macmillan Co., 1951) 135.

[9]*Chambers Biographical Dictionary*, ed. Camilla Rockwood (Edinburgh: Chambers Harrap Publishers Ltd., 2007), 767.

[10]Louis Patrick, Presbyterian pastor in Charlotte, North Carolina, related the sound of the apple branches with the call of Frederick Buechner to the ministry, *Protestant Hour*, WSB radio, Atlanta, Georgia.

[11]A. W. Tozer, *The Pursuit of God* (Camp Hill, PA: Christian Publications, Inc., 2009), 82-83.

CHAPTER 18

BEYOND CHANGE ...
We're Not in Kansas Anymore

Acts 1:6-8

Lord, will you at this time restore the kingdom to Israel?
—Acts 1:6

On the cusp of a new millennium, the Alban Institute convened a conference in Louisville, Kentucky, titled "The Church of the Twenty-first Century." Alban Institute of Washington, D.C., is the Mayo Clinic of ministry. On the cutting edge of research, Alban strives to read the signs of the times, and measures the church's vital signs. Pastors converged on the conference hungry, even desperate, for a prognosis on the church's future. But despite a montage of materials, the conferees came away with only one certainty, not about the future, but about the past: "We're not in Kansas anymore."

That declaration belongs to Dorothy in Frank Baum's classic film, *The Wizard of Oz*. Following a Kansas cyclone, Dorothy and three friends—Scarecrow, Tin Man, and Lion—trudge the yellow brick road in search of the Wizard, whom they believe has power to fulfill their deepest desires. Dorothy, of course, desires a way back to Kansas, which lies "somewhere over the rainbow."

Unlike the wizard of Oz, with his smoke and mirrors, the wise men of Alban confess that they see the church's future "in a mirror, dimly" (1 Cor. 13:12a). Only one conviction is clear: We're not in Kansas anymore. Furthermore, there is no way back. Therefore, we face a challenge: How shall we endure this dislocation following the cyclone of change called postmodernity?[1]

The Way We Were

Kansas is more than a place on the map located in the heart of America's breadbasket. Kansas is a mythical place of collective memories and stories similar to Garrison Keelor's "Lake Wobegon," where "all the men are handsome, and all the women are strong, and all the children are above average."

Perhaps another name for Kansas is Camelot, defined as a place, time, or circumstance characterized by idealized beauty, peacefulness, and enlightenment. The memory of Camelot evokes the song:

> Don't let it be forgot
> That once there was a spot,
> For one brief, shining moment,
> That was known as Camelot.[2]

For the Englishman, Camelot was the place and reign of King Arthur and his knights of the Roundtable. It was the age of chivalry, honor, and nobility. It was a time when men and women remained "loyal to the royal" that resided from within themselves. Camelot endures in collective memories, even though it never fully existed in reality.

For Jewish persons, Camelot was the golden age of King David and the twelve tribes of Israel. Furthermore, the apostles of Jesus remembered his promise to restore that period of the past in a future of political domination: "Assuredly I say to you, that in the regeneration, when the Son of Man sits on the throne of his glory, you who have followed me will also sit on twelve thrones, judging the twelve tribes of Israel" (Matt. 19:28).

In a state of blind ambition the apostles were ready to take office and rule. Thus, their question to the risen Lord before his ascension into glory: "Lord is it at this time you are restoring the kingdom to Israel?" (Acts 1:6b). Would Jesus use his resurrection power to turn the calendar back a millennium and restore Israel's golden age—as John D. Rockefeller, Jr. used his wealth to restore colonial Williamsburg?

Surely the apostles were disappointed when the Lord replied: "It is not for you to know the times or seasons which the Father has put in his own authority" (Acts 1:7). The future of the church cannot be predicted nor her past re-created. We're not in Kansas anymore.

But perhaps a better word for Kansas is Christendom. The origin of Christendom can be traced to the battle of Milvian Bridge on the banks of the Tiber River in Rome. There, on October 28, 312 A.D., Constantine marched his army against the Roman emperor, Maxentius. On the eve of battle, Constantine saw a vision of Greek letters written across the sky and heard a voice telling him, "In this sign, you shall conquer." This was the sign of the Christian God. Constantine prevailed, became emperor of the empire, and legally declared Christianity as the official religion. For the remainder of its existence, the Roman Empire would be "Christian." State funds would build churches; pagans would be persecuted; the church would become wealthy—and corrupt.[3] Historians would label this age in which church and state were one as the Dark Ages.

And yet, some of us grew up in a time of religious consensus and family values reminiscent of the age of Christendom. Local political institutions propped up the programs of the church. Those were the days when "the belfries of all Christendom"[4] still peeled their evening vespers downtown across Main Street's public square, and the public square was still decorated during seasons of the year with Christian symbols. There were spiritual giants in the land in those days of Christian consensus.

One day at Sunday lunch an elderly hostess asked if I had ever heard preach the famed pastor of Dallas, Texas, Doctor Marshall Craig. Ironically, I heard Marshall Craig preach once in chapel at Clearwater, Florida, when I was a sophomore in high school. If Kansas were the latch on America's breadbasket, Clearwater was the buckle on the Bible Belt.

Doctor Craig was conducting revival services at Calvary Church located downtown, a few blocks from Clearwater High. Mr. William Feagan, our principle and also a deacon at Calvary Church, ordered the faculty and student body to report to chapel on a given day and give our attention to the visiting evangelist. There, the preacher winsomely confronted his audience with the compelling claims of Christ—and no one filed a lawsuit!

Christendom, or at least the Christian consensus, still prevailed. Blue laws enforced Sunday closings to keep the 11 a.m. worship hour safe from competition. Beloved war hero, General Dwight Eisenhower, was in the White House and added to our national pledge the phrase, "under God," to keep the country safe from Communism. The preacher and the bootlegger—the original odd couple—worked for different reasons to keep the county dry and safe from liquor. And, Mr. Feagan kept the chapel safe for visiting evangelists. Those were the days of Christendom, or at least the Christian consensus. We thought they would never end. But they did.

Forty years later, a tornado touched down in Clearwater while the city slept. Palm trees and rooftops were blown away; flash floods deposited oil slicks on the well-manicured suburban paradise. Some of us summoned back to Clearwater to attend to damaged houses empty now except for memories felt like Dorothy: we're not in Clearwater any-more—not the Clearwater we had known and loved.

Things other than palm trees and rooftops are missing there. Evangelists no longer preach in chapel at Clearwater High. There is no chapel. There are security checkpoints and armed policemen. Calvary Church still soldiers on downtown. But a few blocks away the old Fort Harrison Hotel is now owned by a religious cult headquartered in Hollywood, California. The cult appeals to film stars, celebrities, young professionals, and especially young people. Some believe this cult has impacted young people numerically and psychologically more than the youth programs of all the churches of the city combined.

We're not in Christendom anymore. There exists no Christian consensus. Perhaps we are like the devout woman who broke her crucifix and exclaimed, "Now, I shall have to trust God alone!"[5]

Back to the Future

If we are not in Kansas anymore, or in Camelot, or in Christendom, where are we? We are figuratively in Jerusalem. We are back to the future.

Mark Twain believed that history does not repeat, but it does rhyme. The ponderings of the twenty-first-century church at Louisville, Kentucky, rhymes with the probing of the first-century church at Jerusalem: Lord, is it at this time you are restoring the kingdom of Israel? Neither church can return to the past, but both churches can enter the future armed with a story to tell to the nations: "But you shall receive power when the Holy Spirit has come upon you; and you shall be my witnesses to me in Jerusalem, and in all Judea and Samaria, and to the end of the earth" (Acts 1:8).

Following the Ascension, after the Lord is lifted up, his disci-ples will receive power to speak up. Ours is not the power of political domination, but rather the persuasive power of articulation. The Holy Spirit enables this ministry of articulation to Christ's witnesses. The Spirit gives courage to speak, "for we cannot but speak the things we have seen and heard" (Acts 4:20). To their hearers, the Spirit gives clarity to understand: "Do you understand what you are reading?" (Acts 8:29).

Therefore, from Jerusalem to Rome—the launching place to the remotest parts of the earth—the disciples tell the story of Jesus and his love. Commenting on the story of Jesus, with its parables, prayers, and personalities, Christian author Christopher Thompson concludes: "I find in these narratives not confirmation of myself, but the very constitution of myself. I do not place the actions of God within the horizon of my story. Rather, I place my story within the actions of God."[6]

The story of Jesus continues, and men and women still locate within that story both their identity and mission.

In a Sunday morning broadcast from the First Presbyterian Church over WSB Radio in Atlanta, Tom Long, professor of preaching at Emory University, told of finding himself in the story. As a boy he often visited his grandmother at the old home place in South Carolina. One day, while poking around the parlor, he noticed on a wall in the midst of the family photographs a Union soldier dressed in blue amid Confederate gray. "Granny, who is the soldier in the blue uniform?" he asked. She replied, "I'll tell you some day when you're old enough to understand."

During a later visit, his curiosity aroused, Tom asked: "Granny, who is the soldier in the blue uniform?" She then told him the story: "The soldier was a chaplain in the Union army. After the battle of Williamsburg in Virginia, he rode out across the battlefield and saw a wounded Confederate soldier lying in a ditch. A minnieball had shattered his kneecap. He was slowly bleeding to death. Dismounting, the chaplain applied a tourniquet to stop the bleeding. Then he carried the soldier back to his own lines and a field hospital where surgeons amputated his leg and saved his life. Later, the chaplain raised money and sent the soldier home to his anxious parents. The Union chaplain's name was Pritchall. The Confederate soldier was your great-grandfather. Had it not been for Pritchall, you wouldn't be here today."

Tom Long, upon reflection, found in that story not the confirmation of himself, but the very constitution of himself. Now he understood the meaning of the word grace, as sung in the famous hymn by John Newton: "Tis grace hath brought me safe thus far, and grace will lead me home."

We're not in Kansas anymore; neither are we in Camelot or Christendom. We're not with Dorothy and her friends on the yellow brick road; we are with Jesus and his friends on the narrow way that leads to life. Our journey will take us not to the Emerald City, but to the New Jerusalem. Jesus not only knows the way home, but he is home.

A Promise

> To an open house in the evening
> Home shall men come,
>
> To an older place than Eden
> And a taller town than Rome;
>
> To the end of the way
> Of the wandering star,
>
> To the things that cannot be
> And that are,
>
> The place where God was homeless
> And all men are at home.
>
> —G. K. Chesterton[7]

A Prayer

> O God, in the fog and fury of this dark age, keep the inner world of heart and mind in us clear and strong, that we may not be buffeted from our course by the wild winds or chaos and seas of bitterness. Help us onward through all kinds of weather to follow patiently the north star of [your] eternal purpose and, if darkness and chaos hide it, hold us firm by every remembrance and hope to do [your] will through Jesus Christ our Lord. Amen.
>
> —Samuel H. Miller[8]

Notes

¹Historians use events as figurative bookends of the modern period: The modern period lies between the fall of the Bastille and the beginning of the French Revolution in 1789 and the fall of the Berlin Wall in 1989.

²Alan J. Learner, *The Oxford Dictionary of Quotations*, ed. Elizabeth Knowles (New York: Oxford University Press, 1999), 465.

³Rufus Fears, *The World Was Never the Same: Events That Changed History* (Chantilly, VA: The Great Courses, 2010), 33-34.

⁴From the 1864 hymn by Henry W. Longfellow, "I Heard the Bells on Christmas Day."

⁵I believe this expression was recorded by David Buttrick in *Homiletic: Moves and Structures* (Philadelphia: Fortress Press, 1987).

⁶Quoted by Charles J. Chaput, O.F.M., archbishop of Denver, in Christopher James Thompson, *Christian Doctrines, Christian Identity: Augustine and the Narratives of Character* (Lanham, MD: University Press of America, 1999), 99.

⁷G. K. Chesterton, "The House of Christmas," quoted in James S. Stewart, *A Faith to Proclaim* (New York: Charles Scribner's Sons, 1953), 11.

⁸Samuel H. Miller, *What Child Is This? Readings and Prayers for Advent/Christmas* (Philadelphia: Fortress Press, 1982), 21.

CHAPTER 19

BEYOND THE DOGS OF WAR ...
Private Ryan and the Young Prince of Glory

Romans 5:1-8

Cry "Havoc!," and let slip the dogs of war.
—William Shakespeare[1]

The twenty-first century has already been labeled "the century of the woman."[2] If I were asked to name the twentieth century, I would call it "the century of the soldier," for it marked the bloodiest hundred years in the history of humankind. The soldier stood awash in the "blood-dimmed tide" that drenched the earth in human misery. Our national debt to the citizen soldier is beyond measure.

The soldier's story has been told in three unforgettable films: *Sergeant York* is the hero who hated war. *Patton* is the hero who loved war. *Private Ryan* is the hero who was reluctantly delivered from war. *Sergeant York* and *Patton* are entertaining; *Private Ryan* is heart-wrenching. But the word is "catharsis," for the story offers a form of cleansing. In his masterful film, Steven Spielberg portrays a simple but troubling question: Is the life of one man worthy of the deaths of so many?

The story begins in a cemetery in Normandy. The Stars and Stripes wave in a gentle sea breeze above long columns of white crosses marking the graves of the fallen. An elderly man kneels before a cross-beam and reads the inscription:

Captain John Miller / Ranger, Pennsylvania / June 14, 1944

The kneeling man is Francis Ryan, accompanied at a distance by his wife, children, and grandchildren. Suddenly he begins to sob. When his wife anxiously approaches, he says imploringly, "Tell me . . . tell me I'm a good man!"

"You are," she whispers. "You are."

Francis Ryan has measured his long life against the memories of those who died fifty years earlier.

In the movie, Ryan, one of four sons from an Iowa farm, parachutes into France on D-Day. Unknown to him, but known to General Marshall and his staff, Ryan's three brothers have been killed in action. General Marshall orders that he be found and sent home. The staff protests. Risks to the rescuers are too great—and unjustified. The general counters by quoting a poignant letter written to a mother who reportedly lost five sons in another theatre of war:

> I pray that our Heavenly Father may assuage the anguish
> of your bereavement and leave you only the cherished
> memory of the loved and lost, and the solemn pride
> that must be yours to have laid so costly a sacrifice upon
> the altar of freedom.
>
> Executive Mansion, A. Lincoln[3]

While they speak, a mother in Iowa washes the breakfast dishes and looks through her kitchen window at a spiral of dust rising from the dirt road approaching the farm. The dust is created by an Army staff car bearing an officer and a minister who have come with the solemn news that she has laid three sons on the altar of freedom. Her only surviving son is somewhere in France—at risk. Meanwhile in Washington, General Marshall's tone is imperious: "I want Private Ryan found and sent home!"

Hours later, Captain John Miller and a squad of brave men begin their perilous search for Private Ryan. Casualities mount. An enemy sniper hidden in a bell tower, a machine gun nest concealed in a cow pasture, take a terrible toll. One by one the number of the squad diminishes as the men are devoured by the dogs of war. With each appalling loss, the survivors measure the worth of the sacrifice.

"This guy Ryan, wherever he is," says one soldier, "had better invent the world's greatest light bulb!"

But how many light bulbs or inventions by one man could make up for the sacrifice of so many?

Private Ryan is eventually found, but the remnant of his rescuers is lost. Final deliverance follows a bloody battle on a bridge where human flesh stands against raw steel. When the guns are silent, Ryan bends over the mortally wounded Captain Miller, who utters two words: "Earn it. Earn it."

Freedom purchased by the dying must be earned by the living. And so, fifty years later an elderly man remembers and weeps and wonders if he had really earned it.

"Tell me I'm a good man!"

The film ends. But its mood and message remain. Outside the theatre the shopping mall is empty. Nearby restaurants are gorged with revelers. Affluent and bored youth cruise the parking lot, their boom boxes blaring. Fifty years ago young men their age were landing and dying on the beaches of Normandy. Would they do it again?

The film's message makes you wonder, in this land of the free, what kind of people have we become? From the New York Island to the Redwood Forest, our land is honeycombed with clusters of hatred. The barbarians are no longer at our frontiers; the enemy is within. As the philosopher Pogo put it: "We have met the enemy, and he is us!"

The germs of intolerance and bigotry have bred in our body politic a malignant rage. For its cure we shall have to turn to another soldier and an ancient sacrifice.

For the Christian, those crosses in the cemetery at Normandy rekindle memories of another cross—on a hill far away—on which the Prince of Glory died. The inscription on the crossbeam was written in Hebrew, Latin, and Greek: "Jesus King of the Jews" (Matt. 27:37).

Earlier, Jesus prepared his men for his approaching death: "From that time Jesus began to show his disciples that he must go to Jerusalem and suffer many things from the elders and chief priests and scribes, and be killed, and on the third day be raised" (Matt. 16:21). At Jesus' trial the high priest packed into one terse sentence the necessity of his sacrifice: "It is expedient that one man should die for the sins of the people" (John 18:14b). But are the people worth it?

Private Ryan evokes the question: Is the life of one man worthy of the deaths of so many? But the young Prince of Glory reverses the question: Are the lives of the many worth the death of one man?

The apostle Paul ponders the character of those for whom others offer the supreme sacrifice. For what kind of person will another dare to die? A righteous person? A good person? Perhaps for a good man, like Francis Ryan, someone like Captain Miller will voluntarily lay down his life. But the astounding fact is, "while we were yet sinners, Christ died for us." That is one of the most incredible sentences in all of Scripture. Before we were "worthy" or "righteous" or "good" or could invent the world's greatest light bulb, Christ died for us.

After all, character labels are risky. The Hebrew poet following an inquest into the human heart concluded, "There is none righteous, no not one" (Rom 3:10). Even Jesus, in whom the most searching moral inquiry of the ages found no fault, disclaimed the label "good."

In response to the rich young ruler who asked, "Good Master, what must I do to inherit eternal life?" Jesus replied, "Why do you call me good? There is none good but one, that is God" (Matt. 19:17).

In his cast of characters, Doctor Luke portrays an exemplary Roman soldier seeking healing for his servant. The community commends him to Jesus with the words, "He is worthy."

But he wins the Master's admiration with the simple confession, "I am not worthy" (Luke 7:4, 6).

And neither are we!

To be sure, such a modest conclusion about character may injure self-esteem. For some, sin is a poor self-image and salvation is the recovery of self-esteem. Many are convinced the ills that bedevil the community with violence and drugs are because people think too ill of themselves.

A community in Massachusetts once anxiously debated the wisdom of continuing the spelling bee because children who misspelled a word often wept. Their self-esteem had been shattered by failure. But what if they misspell life? There was also talk of ending Little League because children who came up to bat often struck out. But did not Babe Ruth set a record for strikeouts? Church folk call for a new reformation of self-esteem. But Jesus called for reformation of self-denial.

Does not worthy living begin with the recognition that we are unworthy? And does not life confirm, "Whoever humbles himself is the greatest in the kingdom of heaven" (Matt. 18:4)?

According to a story of tradition, when a group of American tourists in Europe were shown a piano on which Beethoven composed his master works, a frivolous young girl ran over to the instrument and played "Chopsticks." The crowd applauded. The guide said, "That's interesting that you should do that. Last week we had in here Paderewski, the great concert artist." "I'll bet he did what I just did," said the young woman. "No," responded the guide, "he didn't. The people tried to persuade him to play something, but he refused and said, 'I'm not worthy'."

And neither are we.

So in the flight of imagination, I return like Francis Ryan to the place of sacrifice. I climb the hill of Calvary and kneel beneath the cross on which the Prince of Glory died. Searing self-examination evokes the question: Am I a good man? Then I remember: only one is good.

I hear the whisper of the last words from the cross: not "Earn it," but rather "It is finished!" (John 19:30b).

My freedom in Christ is not a deliverance to be achieved but a gift to be received. The gift is named "grace." I come away aware that I can never invent the world's greatest light bulb, but I can reflect the light of the world.

And so can you.

A Prayer

What did you see, soldier? What did you see at the war?

I saw such glory and horror as I've never seen before,
I saw men's hearts burned naked in red crucibles of pain;
I saw such Godlike courage as I'll never see again.

What did you pray, soldier? What did you pray at war?

I prayed that we might do the thing we have not done before; that we might mobilize for peace—nor mobilize in vain lest Christ and man be forced to climb stark Calvary again.

—Don Blanding[4]

Notes

[1]From *Julius Caesar*, act 3, scene 1.

[2]Attributed to R. Kirby Godsey, chancellor, Mercer University, Macon, Georgia.

[3]Elton Trueblood, *Abraham Lincoln: Theologian of American Anguish* (New York: Harper & Row Publishers, 1973), 74.

[4]Don Blanding, "A Prayer," *A Soldier's War Experience*, wikipedia.org/wiki/Don Blanding.

Evening on Karl Johan Street
Edvard Munch, 1892
© 2012 The Munch Museum/ The Munch-Ellingsen Group/Artists Rights Society
(ARS) New York.

These denizens of Christiania (today's Oslo) appear
to be ghouls, the walking dead parallel to Thoreau's
contemptuous reference to "the mass of men [who] lead
lives of quiet desperation." Munch's special citizens seem
risen from the dead, like some kind of last judgment
where the dead resurface and put on frock coats and
top hats and fine gowns, while the remaining dazed
mannequins move in mass formation, but willless and
soulless . . . This, too, is a community . . . a whole class
of like-minded, like-appareled citizens, aware of the
surface features that unite them, wholly unaware of the
inner void that unites them. [This] is an urbane portrait
of hell, not the fiery traditional hell we usually imagine,
but the icy hell of erasure and nullity. Could any of us
have seen this, had we been on the Karl Johan?

—adapted from Arnold Weinstein,
A Scream Goes Through the House:
What Literature Teaches Us About Life

CHAPTER 20

BEYOND THE CROWD ...
Quo Vadis?

Matthew 7:13-14

*Narrow is the gate and difficult is the way which leads to life, and there
are few who find it.*

—*Matthew 7:14*

Quo Vadis? (Where are you going?) That was the last question a minister asked Henry David Thoreau (1817-1862) as Thoreau lay on his
deathbed. Thoreau, who built a shanty in the woods near Walden Pond
in Massachusetts, where he became a writer and partial recluse, replied:
"One world at a time please!"[1]

The question was urgent. The answer was probably not flippant.
It reflects a sequential investment of life in the world, as if earth comes
first and heaven comes after it.[2] If in Thoreau's mind, there is a heaven.
But the sequential approach of one world at a time may ultimately mean
the loss of both worlds.

Quo Vadis? (Where are you going?) is perhaps the foremost religious question for all discussion and comparison. "The end," wrote T.
S. Eliot "is where we start from."[3] All founders of faith and all systems
of belief owe their inquirers an explanation of their aims. If I follow this
particular pathway, where will it end? To what destiny does it lead?

Arrival

At the conclusion of the Sermon on the Mount, Jesus confronts his hearers with the end: "Enter by the straight gate; for the gate is wide that

leads to destruction . . . for the gate is strait . . . that leads to life" (Matt. 5:13-14).

In biblical imagery the gate stands not at the beginning of the journey, but at the end—the final entrance into the temple, the city, or the kingdom of heaven.[4]

The psalmist has composed a liturgy that accompanies the long procession of King David and his arrival at the temple of Jerusalem, bearing the Ark of the Covenant containing the Ten Commandments, symbolizing the victory of God over the forces of chaos (2 Sam. 6:12-19). At the temple gates the procession stops and a choir addresses the temple gates as if they were persons: "Lift up your heads, O gates, and be lifted up, O ancient doors, and the King of Glory can come in!"

Then, voices from within reply: "Who is the King of Glory?" And those outside then cry out: "The Lord strong and mighty, the Lord mighty in battle."

A second time the singers outside call on the gates to lift, and voices from within repeat the question: "Who is the King of Glory?"

Then comes the answer that will unlock the gates: "The Lord of Hosts, he is the King of Glory!" (Ps. 24:7-10). Suddenly, the gates open. The procession enters. The journey is ended. The Lord reigns. Similarly, John the seer envisions the descent of the Holy City and the arrival of the redeemed: "And I saw no temple in it, for the Lord God, the Almighty, and the Lamb, are its temple . . . and the nations shall walk by its light, and the kings of the earth shall bring their glory into it. And in the daytime (for there shall be no night there) its gates shall never be closed" (Rev. 21:22-26).

James Michener captures the mood of these texts of arrival in the relief of medieval pilgrims who traveled the long road from France to the Cathedral of Saint Thomas in Spain. As they neared the end of their demanding journey, their eyes strained toward the horizon, hoping to see the towers of the long-sought cathedral in the distance. The first one to see would shout, "My joy! My joy! My joy!"[5] Similarly, Jesus, in one of the parables of the kingdom, says to the faithful, "Enter into the joy of your Lord" (Matt. 25:21).

Consequently, Jesus confronts his hearers with a question that once hung as a banner across Main Street in a small western town: "If you get to where you are going, where will you be?"[6]

Ethical

Quo Vadis? ("Where are you going?") evokes a companion question: "With whom are you going?"

"The way is broad that leads to destruction, and many are those who enter it. For the way is narrow that leads to life, and few are those who find it" (Matt. 17:13-14). Matthew's Jesus consistently contrasts the character of the many and the few: "For many are called, but few are chosen" (Matt. 22:14). Matthew further extracts the ethical from eschatology (the study of last things). Righteousness is placed next to the Kingdom of God: "But seek first his kingdom and his righteousness, and all these things shall be added to you" (Matt. 6:33).

Robert Frost told us how life-changing a journey down the uncommon road can be: "I took the [road] less traveled by, and that has made all the difference."

But what difference does the narrow way traveled by the few really make? The difference lies in its difficulty. The company of the committed are few in number because the way to the gates of glory is hard.

Sam Rayburn, former Speaker of the House of Representatives in Washington, D.C., used to advise congressional freshmen: "The best way to get along is to go along."[7] That is the easy way for those who are along for the ride. But where does it end? The easy way often ends in disappointment, disbarment, or disgrace. That is one of the perils of living in one world at a time.

The pilgrims who trudge the narrow way believe in "two worlds at a time." They relate the two worlds, earth and heaven, not sequentially but rather simultaneously, as if the eternal world above invades and interpenetrates the temporal world below.[8]

A television station in Louisiana sent a reporter to interview a remarkable woman who all by herself managed to feed, clothe, and educate eight children in a bayou tarpaper shack. "What kept you going in spite of the odds?" was the question. "I seen," she said, "I seen a new world coming."[9]

Hers is a bipolar faith[10] in which the kingdom of God and his righteousness interpenetrate the Louisiana bayou and its realities. The people who live in two worlds at a time make all the ethical difference in this one.

Visible

Quo Vadis? ("Where are you going?") is a question borne of metaphor, a word that carries us across the abyss separating the invisible from the visible. All writers of Scripture are masters of metaphor, and all metaphors of Scripture point to the Master. "I am the way" is not a place in asphalt or lines on a map, but a person alongside. "The way to heaven is heaven," quipped Dorothy Day, "because Jesus said, 'I am the way.'"[11]

Notice that all biblical metaphors of passage—ways, gates, doors—have one fact in common: they remain open.

• The Good Shepherd declares himself a revolving door through whom souls go "in and out" to luxuriate in green pastures and repose by still waters (John 10:3, 7, 9).
• The spirit of Christ constructs in the architecture of the faithful church an open door that no one can shut (Rev. 3:8).
• The final vision of heaven portrays a gated community of eternal security, but whose gates shall never be closed (Rev. 21:5b).

But if the portals to paradise remain open, why do so few pass through them? "Because narrow is the gate and difficult is the way which leads to life, and there are few who find it" (Matt. 7:14).

Sandy Ray, popular Brooklyn pastor remembered for his concrete images, used to advise his hearers: "Always drive in the right lane, so you won't miss the exit sign."[12] Matthew's Jesus adds: and with the right person. "Lo I am with you always, even to the end of the age" (Matt. 28:20).

Will we have grace to face our final exit gracefully? The Christian consensus is yes, when we need it. A boat is needed only when you come to the river; a graceful exit is provided when you come to the exit.

On a cold night in December, during a medical crisis, I rode Amtrak's Number 2100 from Manassas, Virginia, to Gainesville, Georgia. My wife had fallen down a flight of stairs and had undergone emergency surgery for a broken hip.

Upon boarding the train I was greeted by the conductor, a young woman, who asked one question: *Quo Vadis?* (Where are you going?) Whereupon, I was assigned a seat and my destination written on a card and pinned above the luggage rack. "In the morning," said she, "a crew member will appear and assist you off the train. Good night."

It was a restless night. Sleep was intermittent, interrupted by the rhythms of the rails. Hours later, Number 2100 kept a rendezvous with the Chattahoochee River, tumbling "out of the hills of Habersham, down through the valley of Hall," racing past hamlets with dilapidated depots and Christmas decorations hung above the darkened streets.

The scenes outside the window seemed surreal. Telephone poles appeared upside down as if they were bouncing off the cars and hurdling into space. I felt panic-stricken: I don't know where we are. What if I can't get off the train? Suddenly, there was a hand on my shoulder. A crew member had appeared as promised. "Get your things together," she said. "It will soon be time to get off the train." She escorted me down the aisle as the train slowed and then stopped. Steel doors flung open; she alighted onto a portable platform and helped me down. "You're home, now," she said. "Goodbye and good luck."

Whereupon, she reboarded the train whose doors slammed shut, the diesel surged, and Number 2100 disappeared into the twilight.

So the gospel story ends with a promise: Someone will appear to help you with a graceful exit when you reach the final exit. Thus we pray in anticipation of the Presence: "You hold me by my right hand. You will guide me with your counsel, and afterward receive me to glory" (Ps. 73:23b-24).

A Prayer

It is by the goodness of God that we were brought into this world. It is by the grace of God that we have been kept until this very hour. And it is by the love of God, revealed in the face of Jesus, that we are being redeemed. Amen.

—John Claypool[13]

Notes

[1]Peter Kreft, *Making Sense Out of Suffering* (Cincinatti: Servant Books, 1986), 171.

[2]William E. Hull, *Harbingers of Hope* (Tuscaloosa: University of Alabama Press, 2007), 244.

[3]T. S. Eliot, *Little Gidding,* no. 4 of "Four Quartets," www.goodreads.com/quotes.

[4]Ulrich Luz, *Matthew 1-7, A Commentary* (Minneapolis: Fortress Press, 1989), 435.

[5]Thomas Long, *Hebrews,* Interpretation: A Biblical Commentary for Teaching and Preaching (Louisville: John Knox Press, 1997), 119.

[6]Quoted at a noon service at First Baptist Church of Griffin, Georgia, by Randall Lolly, former pastor of First Baptist Church, Winston-Salem, North Carolina.

[7]President John F. Kennedy, freshman congressman from Massachusetts, remembered this quotation by Rayburn. Source unknown.

[8]Hull, 244.

[9]David Buttrick, *Preaching Jesus Christ* (Philadelphia: Fortress Press, 1988), 52.

[10]Hull, 244.

[11]Eugene Peterson, *The Jesus Way* (Grand Rapids: Wm. B. Eerdmans Publishing, 2007), 41.

[12]Gardner Taylor delivered the eulogy for Sandy F. Ray, "A President of Preaching," *The Words of Gardner Taylor: Special Occasion and Expository Sermons* (Valley Forge, PA: Judson Press, 2004), 138-143. Somewhere Taylor attributes this quote to Ray.

[13]The late John Claypool, Episcopal priest, pastor, author, and teacher, often dismissed his congregations with this benediction.

For now we see through a mirror dimly, but then face to face.
—1 Corinthians 13:12

Study for the Cross and the World
Thomas Cole, 1846
Picture courtesy of the Bridgeman Art Library.